Sustainable Urban Transitions and
New Public Management

Kristin Reichborn-Kjennerud

Sustainable Urban Transitions and New Public Management

The Norwegian Experience

Kristin Reichborn-Kjennerud
The Work Research Institute
OsloMet – Oslo Metropolitan University
Oslo, Norway

ISBN 978-3-031-82306-0   ISBN 978-3-031-82307-7 (eBook)
https://doi.org/10.1007/978-3-031-82307-7

© The Editor(s) (if applicable) and The Author(s), under exclusive license to Springer Nature Switzerland AG 2025

This work is subject to copyright. All rights are solely and exclusively licensed by the Publisher, whether the whole or part of the material is concerned, specifically the rights of reprinting, reuse of illustrations, recitation, broadcasting, reproduction on microfilms or in any other physical way, and transmission or information storage and retrieval, electronic adaptation, computer software, or by similar or dissimilar methodology now known or hereafter developed.

The use of general descriptive names, registered names, trademarks, service marks, etc. in this publication does not imply, even in the absence of a specific statement, that such names are exempt from the relevant protective laws and regulations and therefore free for general use.

The publisher, the authors and the editors are safe to assume that the advice and information in this book are believed to be true and accurate at the date of publication. Neither the publisher nor the authors or the editors give a warranty, expressed or implied, with respect to the material contained herein or for any errors or omissions that may have been made. The publisher remains neutral with regard to jurisdictional claims in published maps and institutional affiliations.

Cover illustration: Pattern © Melisa Hasan

This Palgrave Macmillan imprint is published by the registered company Springer Nature Switzerland AG.
The registered company address is: Gewerbestrasse 11, 6330 Cham, Switzerland

If disposing of this product, please recycle the paper.

Acknowledgements

I would like to thank the participants of the Democratic Urban Development in the Digital Age project (DEMUDIG—project no. 281131, funded by the Research Council of Norway) for a good and inspiring research collaboration from fall 2018 to spring 2022. I would also like to extend special thanks to Tereza Østbø Kuldova, who gave me invaluable help in setting the book into the right form. Thanks to Sveinung Legard, Bhavna Middah, Ian McShane, and José Manuel Ruano de la Fuente for the data collection, and Thor Martin Bakke deserves gratitude for helping me analyse the data. Many thanks to Frøja Storm-Mathisen, Eivind Falkum, and Sissel Hovik for reading through the draft and providing solid input. Warm thoughts are also sent to all the informants who shared their experiences on how they have worked for better living conditions and increased social sustainability in their local environments.

Contents

1 Introduction: New Public Management and the Hollowing Out of the Notion of Sustainability — 1

2 Towards Socially Sustainable Community Development — 7

3 The Origins and Main Tools of New Public Management — 21

4 New Public Management in Education, Working Life, and Public Procurement — 37

5 New Public Management in Urban Governance — 51

6 The Sustainable City: Barriers and Enablers — 73

7 How to Create Socially Sustainable Places — 109

8 Solutions for the Future — 125

Index — 139

About the Author

Kristin Reichborn-Kjennerud Research professor Kristin Reichborn-Kjennerud is a political scientist and sociologist and is now working on the topic of sustainability.

She has been engaged in several projects on urban governance and development. Her research interests are democracy and the organization for co-decision-making in urban regeneration processes. She is also interested in urban governance related to social innovation and the quality of government. She was work package leader in a recent project financed by the Norwegian Research Council (NRC) on urban governance, participatory democracy, and ICT (DEMUDIG). She was project leader in a project on sustainable public procurement of food and catering services financed by the Norwegian Research Council, and also work package leader in the EdiCitNet Horizon project on implementing nature-based solutions from For-runner to Follower cities in Living Labs, using governance and evaluation frameworks to make cities more socially and environmentally sustainable. These last two projects are concerned with the unsustainability of the current food system.

Kristin's earlier work has been on evaluation, control, and accountability. She has published extensively in international journals on these topics. Her background concerns studies on governance in the public sector, including comparative research on Supreme Audit Institutions.

CHAPTER 1

Introduction: New Public Management and the Hollowing Out of the Notion of Sustainability

Abstract This book's overarching argument is that current New Public Management (NPM) inspired instruments are incompatible with the transition to a more sustainable society. The public sector follows a logic of efficiency and effectiveness in isolated areas, when what the world needs is a more holistic approach. This chapter provides an overview of the book and a brief explanation of the Norwegian experience in adopting NPM principles and instruments. Norway was a late adopter of NPM, and the authorities' strategy has been to open up the public sector as a market rather than to privatize public services. Urban planning and development are used as the main examples of the marketization of public organizations throughout the book, but examples are also given from public health, research, public procurement, education, and working life. Better wellbeing is put forth as an alternative principle for developing our cities.

Keywords New Public Management (NPM) • Sustainable Development Goals (SDGs) • Norway • Marketization of the public sector

© The Author(s), under exclusive license to Springer Nature Switzerland AG 2025
K. Reichborn-Kjennerud, *Sustainable Urban Transitions and New Public Management*,
https://doi.org/10.1007/978-3-031-82307-7_1

Nordic welfare states are often seen as ideals to be emulated. However, over the past 40 to 50 years, these welfare states have been hollowed out by the instruments of New Public Management (NPM), with profound consequences for how we conceive of sustainability. *Sustainable Urban Transitions and New Public Management* is written for all those genuinely invested in creating sustainable futures, while simultaneously struggling to make sense of how and why the progressive hollowing out of the welfare state is undermining these noble goals in practice. I argue that without seriously rethinking contemporary modes of governance, we are unlikely to ever see a sustainable future, even in a country such as Norway, regularly at the top of all sustainability, governance, innovation, and quality of life rankings. The fact that Norway is often portrayed as the "most sustainable country in the world"[1] should not prevent us from a critical interrogation of the realities that do not make it into simplified rankings. While this book uses Norway as a case, the insights it offers as well as its conclusions are likely to resonate across other contexts as well. Why is Norway a particularly interesting case to explore when thinking through the intersection of NPM and sustainability (discourses)? Norway was a late adopter of NPM and the authorities' strategy has been to open up the public sector as a market rather than to privatize public services. Norway is a good example of what the consequences of NPM can be, particularly in countries that have traditionally chosen more collective and collaborative models of governance. This book explores in detail these consequences in the Norwegian context, with an eye to the complex issue of sustainability—the notion of which, I argue, has been hollowed out by the never-ceasing marketization of the state.

This book is interdisciplinary, like the Sustainable Development Goals (SDGs) of the United Nations. As such, it does not fit neatly within only one university discipline. Instead, its aim is to think transversally, focusing on intersections and interconnections, and bridging disciplinary divides, while also creating new pathways. Sociological concepts, such as social capital, political science concepts like governance, gentrification, participation, and NPM, and the concept of community planning are all brought together in order to better understand sustainable urban transitions, with an eye towards a more enlightened debate.

---

[1] "What Puts Nordic Countries at the Top of The Sustainability Rankings?" https://www.activesustainability.com/sustainable-development/nordic-countries-top-sustainability-rankings/?_adin=11734293023

This book will hopefully help readers understand what sustainability really means, and support them in explaining it to others, thereby also becoming a useful tool and point of departure for starting professional discussions. I sincerely hope that this book finds its uses in sociology and the teaching of it, as it demonstrates how social capital can help counter threats from gentrification, and that it will be used in management studies and political science to discuss the different possible control and management architectures and approaches and their likely consequences for sustainability. Or that it will be used in courses on participation in urban governance to discuss what real participation means, how it could be operationalized, and how it relates to local democracy. The book can also be used in urban planning and facilitate discussions and emergence of new perspectives and practices of community planning and participation.

Brief Book Overview

Since the 1970s, the Norwegian state has modernized its public sector. This modernization meant, in practice, a reform of the public sector inspired by the workings of private markets and companies. In other words, it involved opening up the public sector and transforming it in the image of a competitive marketplace. By now, this market-oriented modernization and transformation of the public sector is very advanced and the negative consequences are also far more visible. There are clear indications that too much emphasis has been placed on control, risk, and competition, that standardization and the quest for efficiency and costs-cutting have come at the expense of quality and sustainability, and that this has negatively affected well-being and social cohesion as much as the environment. It is time to rethink the public sector and the nature of public goods if we are to take the goal of social sustainability seriously. We must ask ourselves what social sustainability really means and what kind of a world we want to inhabit. What are the positive visions for our shared future?

The capitalist and neoliberal reality, with its peculiar modes of governance, control, and regulation that we have constructed around us, is often experienced as our only alternative, what Mark Fisher called "capitalist realism" (Fisher, 2009). The tools authorities use today to create the society we want—or rather to control risks and fight what we do not want—in most sectors, are regulatory and compliance-oriented (Kuldova, 2022). While the market is supposed to deliver and comply with this ever-growing regulation, the latter should be seen as part and parcel of the growth of the Norwegian "regulatory state" (Veggeland, 2009, 2010). The market is organized through a so-called purchaser-provider model, regulated by detailed procurement rules and quality systems. Public organizations order goods and services, while private (or subordinate agencies and enterprises) deliver the services. What is delivered and how, is regulated through detailed contracts. While the old Weberian law- and rule-governed bureaucracy still exists in the public sector, an extra layer of administration is now added to handle contract management—a rapidly expanding and increasingly complex task.

In order to understand the consequences of this model, this book zooms in on urban development, but also provides examples from public health, research, public procurement, education, and working life. It relies on empirical data collected from several research projects: one on participation in urban development, a Horizon 2020 innovation project on how municipalities can support social and environmental initiatives in urban development, and the last on sustainable procurement of food and catering. In urban development, for example, the authorities have delegated much of the responsibility to private companies, while retaining, at least on paper, the position of rule-makers. In reality, however, city development is heavily shaped and controlled by private developers and their profit interests. While the responsibility to consider residents' input and opinions as well as take into account the particular qualities and needs of the area is delegated to private developers, it comes as no surprise that residents' wishes and concerns about well-being quickly come into conflict with their profit-motive, and that denizens' voices are thus often heard as rapidly as possible only to be silenced. This phenomenon and mode of regulation is not unique to urban development. To the contrary, market solutions have been chosen as the model for producing goods and services in most areas.

With the "marketization of the state" (Pierre, 1995), politicians give away power not only to the private sector but also to administrative systems, and the results are not always good. For example, in many new housing projects, the apartments are small and cramped, with little space set aside for outdoor areas. And still, there is a pervasive shortage of housing. In urban development, a political measure has been to build more densely to reduce the climate footprint. Compact urban development limits job-home travel and saves arable land (Hanssen et al., 2015), but even though the authorities are pursuing a policy to build more—and densely—it is becoming less accessible for young people and normal wage earners to live in fast-growing cities like Oslo. Maybe we should question whether urban densification helps reduce the risk of a climate crisis. Do we need to think in a radically different way?

A central point of this book is that municipalities, in their community and urban planning, and in line with the Norwegian *Planning and Building Act*,[2] should have better well-being and welfare as goals as these create positive ripple effects in other areas. The book discusses whether we, in an alternative scenario, could prioritize free areas that open up space for initiative and creativity, where residents can get acquainted, support each other, and engage in activities. Research indicates that overconsumption and pollution heat up the globe and can make it uninhabitable. According to the UN, dramatic changes must occur, particularly in cities, as most people live there and an increasing number are moving there.[3] To reverse the trend, we must make fundamental changes in the way we live. Can we let the vision of a more sustainable society guide us? Is it time for real and holistic sustainability thinking? The current solutions, despite often being dressed in the latest sustainability buzzwords, regularly fail us.

Chapter 2 discusses how social sustainability can be understood in urban development and explains how holistic thinking on sustainability conflicts with the key indicator thinking by the marketized state and NPM. Chapter 3 accounts for the historical origins of the NPM concept and explains its main tools. Chapter 4 reflects on how NPM has affected education, the labour market, and public procurement, while Chap. 5 deals with NPM in urban development and the prerequisites for real participation and sustainability. Chapter 6 reflects on alternative ways to develop the city, and how it could be made more sustainable, while Chap. 7 discusses how we can create places that consider people's social needs to a far greater degree and prioritize these over profit, cost-cutting, and efficiency. Finally, Chap. 8 turns to the challenges of letting competition and individualization come at the expense of cooperation, reiterating the need for building alternative visions. A one-sided focus on production and control is deleterious to democracy and well-being. An alternative could be to bring back the collective and public good as a central value, one that does

---

[2] *Planning and Building Act* (2008). https://www.regjeringen.no/en/dokumenter/planning-building-act/id570450/

[3] "Sustainable Cities: Why They Matter," UN, 2018. https://www.un.org/sustainabledevelopment/wp-content/uploads/2018/09/Goal-11.pdf

not suffer at the expense of profit or efficiency. After all, we must take care of nature and each other.

After reading this book, you will gain a better understanding of what social sustainability means, and how it is linked to environmental sustainability and democratic participation in society's various arenas.

References

Fisher, M. (2009). *Capitalist Realism: Is There No Alternative?* Zero Books.

Hanssen, G. S., Hofstad, H., & Saglie, I. L. (Eds.). (2015). *Kompakt byutvikling: Muligheter og utfordringer.* Universitetsforlaget.

Kuldova, T. Ø. (2022). *Compliance-Industrial Complex: The Operating System of a Pre-Crime Society.* Palgrave Pivot.

Pierre, J. (1995). The Marketization of the State: Citizens, Consumers, and the Emergence of the Public Market. In B. Guy Peters & D. J. Savoie (Eds.), *Governance in a Changing Environment* (pp. 55–81). McGill-Queen's University Press. https://doi.org/10.1515/9780773565500-005

Veggeland, N. (2009). *Taming the Regulatory State: Politics and Ethics.* Edward Elgar Publishing Ltd.

Veggeland, N. (2010). *Den nye reguleringsstaten: Idébrytinger og styringskonflikter.* Gyldendal Akademisk.

CHAPTER 2

Towards Socially Sustainable Community Development

Abstract The concept of sustainability presupposes that public organizations see tasks holistically and cross-sectorally, but also that they co-create solutions with local communities and consider sustainability in a geographical and cultural context. This way of thinking nevertheless conflicts with the key performance indicator thinking in New Public Management (NPM). The method of setting goals and asking for reporting on sustainability indicators oversimplifies complex relationships and prevents real societal transitions. In this chapter, we look more closely at the concept of sustainability and link it to governance of the public sector. The first part of the chapter delves into the origin and historical development of the concept of sustainability, which is then problematized and analyzed in light of community planning and development in the municipalities.

Keywords Management by objectives and results • Social sustainability • NPM • Co-governance

Since the 1980s, various governments have introduced new management and control mechanisms in Norway to streamline the public sector. I argue that these reforms have provided a poor basis for cooperation and created challenges for a socially sustainable community development. Instead of

© The Author(s), under exclusive license to Springer Nature Switzerland AG 2025
K. Reichborn-Kjennerud, *Sustainable Urban Transitions and New Public Management*,
https://doi.org/10.1007/978-3-031-82307-7_2

focusing on social sustainability, creativity, innovation, and flexibility, we have an increasingly strong focus on unit-pricing and cost control. Moreover, competition and time pressures have created further barriers for cooperation. These reforms have, over time, radically altered public organizations. No longer delivering services and products themselves, they have been turned into experts in procurement, in purchasing products and services, and thus reduced to managers of contracts. Not only is it immediately obvious that safeguarding the public mission and common good becomes difficult when public institutions are reduced to more or less mere procurement and contract organizations, but these contracts, along with private standards, best practice guidelines, key performance indicators (KPI), and embedded reporting requirements, reduce flexibility and generate an increased need for administration layered on top of the old bureaucracy. The result is the growth and perpetual layering of control systems, accompanied by distribution, delegation, and disavowal of responsibility.

Over the past 200 years, our societies have been transformed through industrialization, increasing consumption, and the distribution of resources and status according to market principles. This development has warmed the globe, polluted the environment, and deepened social and economic inequalities (Piketty, 2014). To reverse this negative trend, the Norwegian government's signal to municipalities is to use the UN's 17 Sustainable Development Goals (SDGs) in their regional, municipal, community, and spatial planning.[1] All UN member states have, to varying degrees, committed to these sustainable development goals, which have come to frame the horizon of our imagination when it comes to sustainability. At the same time, the SDGs are comprehensive, interrelated, and indicator-oriented, making them difficult to understand and implement for municipalities, companies, and other organizations. The metric focus also creates perverse incentives for gaming the numbers. Most importantly, however, social sustainability, while likely key to attaining sustainable societies, is perhaps the least considered and understood dimension of sustainability.

The concept of sustainability first gained international attention through the World Commission on Environment and Development's

---

[1] "National expectations regarding regional and municipal planning 2023–2027," Ministry of Local Government and Regional Development, 20 June 2023. https://www.regjeringen.no/contentassets/d71a3e61e774485fb4a98cab9255e53f/nasjonale_forventninger_en.pdf

report *Our Common Future* (1987).[2] The World Commission, often referred to as the Brundtland Commission, was a working group appointed by the UN Secretary-General and led by Gro Harlem Brundtland, the former Prime Minister of Norway. The report defined sustainable development as seeking "to meet the needs and aspirations of the present without compromising the ability to meet those of the future. Far from requiring the cessation of economic growth, it recognizes that the problems of poverty and underdevelopment cannot be solved unless we have a new era of growth in which developing countries reap larger benefits."[3] Economic growth, despite posing a risk to the environment, has been deemed as central to achieving sustainability. This definition of sustainability and basic premise still underpins the UN approach to sustainable development.

The concept of sustainability is relatively novel, and has roots in social justice, internationalism, and other earlier movements, with a rich history and ideas that have come together in a call for a sustainable development (Bindhulatha & Kumar, 2021; Kainzbauer & Rungruang, 2019). However, the focus on the social dimension of sustainability was not as clear in the Brundtland Commission's report, which was mostly concerned with the environment and economic development. The adjective sustainable suggests that something should be maintained over time, and refers to the ability or power to maintain, endure, or uphold something over time and at a certain level. Sustainability is often linked with the word development, thus reminding us that development must take place within limits, so that limited natural resources become available to sustain future generations. But the concept of sustainability also points us towards the fact that everything is connected to everything else, and towards the need to think holistically: We must think about nature, social life, and the economy when we develop our societies. If anything needs to be maintained, it is precisely the equilibrium between these areas. Without nature, we have a poor starting point for good societies or an economy altogether, and when everything is sacrificed to and subsumed by the goals of profit-making, we destroy both nature and undermine society. Therefore, we

---

[2] "Report of the World Commission on Environment and Development: Our Common Future." https://sustainabledevelopment.un.org/content/documents/5987our-common-future.pdf

[3] "Report of the World Commission on Environment and Development: Our Common Future," p. 39. https://sustainabledevelopment.un.org/content/documents/5987our-common-future.pdf

must work simultaneously on the environment, the economy, and social conditions to create a sustainable future. It is the connection between these three dimensions that determines whether something is sustainable.

The Brundtland Commission's report was followed up by the first UN conference on the environment and development, the Rio conference in Brazil in 1992. The world's leaders met to discuss and reach consensus on how social and economic development should be combined with environmental considerations. The Rio conference adopted a non-binding action plan for the protection of biological diversity and a convention on emissions of hazardous chemicals. The conference initiated further work with a focus on the connection between the environment, poverty, and water supply in poor countries. The most comprehensive document adopted at the conference was *Agenda 21*,[4] a non-binding global work plan for governments, organizations, and the UN. This conference mandated local authorities and municipalities around the world to engage in dialogue with residents, organizations, and businesses. Together, they were to create action plans for sustainable development in their local communities.[5] In Norway, municipalities, county municipalities, and other organizations drafted an agreement at a national conference in 1998 in Fredrikstad to follow up the Rio conference's goal of mobilizing residents and organizations in the development of local action plans (Harvold, 2002). A follow-up conference was organized in Johannesburg in 2002, and then another conference was held in Rio in 2012 (Hofstad, 2013). At the UN's summit in 2012 on sustainable development, the goal was again to achieve consensus on how social and economic development can best be combined with environmental considerations. The conference also resulted in numerous documents, including the three most well-known legally binding conventions: the United Nations Framework Convention on Climate

---

[4] "United Nations Conference on Environment & Development Rio de Janerio, Brazil, 3 to 14 June 1992: AGENDA 21." https://sustainabledevelopment.un.org/content/documents/Agenda21.pdf

[5] See for example the "Guiding Criteria for Local Agenda 21 Work in Norway" (in Norwegian). https://www.regjeringen.no/globalassets/upload/kilde/md/bro/1999/0003/ddd/pdfv/127676-rettkurs.pdf

Change,[6] the Convention on Biological Diversity,[7] and the Convention to Combat Desertification,[8] which have been followed up by other documents.

In order to make the concept of sustainability more concrete, the UN member states adopted and operationalized the three sustainability dimensions further in the 2030 agenda for sustainable development, with its 17 Sustainable Development Goals (SDGs) and 169 sub-goals, in New York in September 2015. The 17 SDGs are a continuation of the United Nations Millennium Development Goals, apply to all countries, and serve as a roadmap for sustainable development, but are not legally binding. Countries commit to varying degrees, but national governments are expected to create their own frameworks to achieve these goals. The striking difference between the UN Millennium Development Goals and the SDGs is that the former relied on a collaboration between nation states and government, while for the latter, the market, private sector, and investors came to be seen as a potential solution to the problem to a far greater extent than ever before, or as a key to SDGs' success. This became manifest both in how the goals were negotiated and presented, and in the methods used for their follow-up (Machin & Liu, 2023).

The challenge with the SDGs and with the overreliance on market-driven solutions is, however, that they mask the inequality-creating systems, structures, and relationships that make it difficult and highly unlikely for individual organizations alone to deliver meaningful solutions. The method of setting goals and asking for reporting on sustainability indicators can oversimplify complex relationships and effectively prevent, rather than contribute to, real solutions (Telleria & Garcia-Arias, 2022), thus trapping us further in the aforementioned capitalist realism. Alas, there are no simple market and technological fixes or magic bullet, and it is not only naïve to believe there are.

The way we currently measure sustainability is indicator-based, but these are neither neutral nor objective. We must always be aware of what is not measured and what the indicators actually consist of (Mair et al., 2018). As it stands, the unsustainable status quo can be far too easily

---

[6] "United Nations Framework Convention on Climate Change," 1992. https://unfccc.int/resource/docs/convkp/conveng.pdf

[7] "Convention on biological diversity," Rio de Janeiro, 5 June 1992. https://treaties.un.org/doc/Treaties/1992/06/19920605%2008-44%20PM/Ch_XXVII_08p.pdf

[8] https://treaties.un.org/doc/Treaties/1996/12/19961226%2001-46%20PM/Ch_XXVII_10p.pdf

preserved and prevailing interests defended even when the reporting looks good on paper. It is perfectly possible to perform well on indicators even if practice remains unchanged (Merry, 2011), as compliance and reporting maps rarely accurately reflect the territory. To the contrary, they are often designed to misrepresent, obfuscate, deny, and defy, adding layers of opacity while being sold as transparent disclosures (Millet & Kuldova, 2024).

Towards a More Holistic Thinking About Sustainability

Sustainable development is one of the main purposes of the Norwegian *Planning and Building Act* of 2008 (Hanssen & Aarsæther, 2018). The Act opens with: "The Act shall promote sustainable development in the best interests of individuals, society and future generations"[9] and it explicitly incorporates the UN's 17 SDGs. According to the law, sustainability is the purpose and should be at the very core of planning. Through a socially sustainable development, municipalities should ideally promote public health, good housing, levelling of social health differences and secure good conditions of upbringing.

The concept of sustainability, as well as the *Planning and Building Act* of 2018, invite us to take on a more holistic thinking that recognizes that all dimensions of modern societies are of importance and key to sustainability.[10] Thinking holistically means that we must consider the consequences of the measures that we implement in various areas, always staying mindful of the whole. This creates obvious dilemmas, which makes it more challenging to find good solutions. Hence, in practice, we often find that the intention of the law is undermined. While the letter of the law may be followed, the holistic ambitions quickly give way to cost-benefit and profit-oriented thinking. But these tensions are in fact also built into the SDGs. While the SDGs may represent or appear as a harmonious whole, upon closer inspection, we find conflicts between the respective goals and sub-goals. Social sustainability, in particular, often ends up neglected as organizations focus most on reporting on environmental considerations,

---

[9] *Planning and Building Act* (2008). https://www.regjeringen.no/en/dokumenter/planning-building-act/id570450/

[10] "Bærekraftsmålene i plannlegging," (SDGs in planning). https://www.regjeringen.no/no/tema/plan-bygg-og-eiendom/plan_bygningsloven/planlegging/fagtema/baerekraft_i_planlegging/id2846205/

which are or can be made to be economically sustainable or profitable. Working to realize sustainability goals in practice should therefore involve making these goal conflicts visible and trying to create synergies between the goals, rather than maintaining a pretence of harmony. Even within a main dimension, such as environmental sustainability, it is often difficult to prioritize. Plastic packaging, for example, one of our era's major pollution challenges, is not biodegradable. At the same time, the use of plastic can reduce food waste as the packaging increases the shelf life of food. What sustainability means in practice depends not only on our visions of the future, but also on what policy area we are talking about and the indicators, goals, and measurement techniques we choose. Again, indicators are not neutral, rather deeply political. What we measure and incentivize shapes the world we inhabit. To take a simple example, an indicator that focuses on the reduction of plastic packaging can affect indicators for food waste. How great the need is for packaging in turn depends on how far the food is transported and how it is stored, adding further layers of sustainability considerations.

While ensuring sustainable urban development is evidently different from implementing measures to produce and buy food more sustainably, sustainable production and the procurement of food have implications for urban development. If local municipalities demand sustainability and buy local and fresh seasonal food, then local businesses can flourish and possibly make it easier for young people to establish themselves in less central areas. Urban developers can, in turn, facilitate the cultivation of food in and around cities, which again has implications for sustainable local production of food and quality of life. Such measures can also be combined with socially sustainable initiatives, such as the inclusion of the unemployed or marginalized. The complexity and the need to think holistically become obvious even when using such a seemingly simple example. What also becomes apparent is that the three dimensions of sustainability can conflict with each other.

Climate and environmental considerations can override social ones, but the former two can also come into conflict. For instance, the development of wind farms can stand in opposition to local community outdoor interests, as wind turbines, despite generating green electricity, can also pollute the visual landscape and block natural movement patterns for animals and humans. Environmental and social sustainability can also, at least in the short term, conflict with economic goals, such as in public procurement. Organic livestock farming and food that is organically grown and produced can be more expensive, but if more people start eating organic foods, the price could go down over time. Another example is electric cars. Their batteries cost a lot, environmentally speaking, to produce, and it is more environmentally friendly to drive a 10-year-old diesel car that is rarely used than to buy a new electric car every three years. At the same time, driving electric cars results in a lower carbon footprint, depending on how the electricity is produced. In the city of Velenje, an hour's drive from the capital Ljubljana in Slovenia, there is a large coal-fired power plant that produces electricity, which helps keep electric cars on the road in our international power system. Child labor and human rights abuses in mineral extraction for batteries, in addition to the destruction of water and the environment in areas where the minerals are extracted, are another concern (Kara, 2023; McKie, 2021). Seeing electric cars as contributing to sustainable development is not straightforward, rather a trade-off between different concerns and interests.

While the concept of sustainability invites us to understand the world more holistically (Hofstad, 2021), thinking holistically is difficult for municipalities and public organizations because there is no common or shared understanding of what sustainability ultimately means. While, for instance, a more plant-based diet and less food waste are generally recommended, what is most sustainable often varies from place to place. This makes it difficult to provide general advice for measures to be taken. Even though some measures can be seen as good in isolation, they may not address the underlying systemic problems with the way we organize society around increasing and accelerating consumption, growth, and waste production (Boye, 2019). Despite years of working towards sustainable development, there are still few guidelines to help the state and municipal organizations to think holistically about and prioritize sustainability in their operations. Organizations and departments have their own performance goals and KPI they must deliver on, and sustainability is not central in these systems. Delivering on economic indicators often overshadows other concerns. The question is how this form of governance and management impacts public organizations' ability to see societal issues holistically and across sectors.

The concept of sustainability not only presupposes that public organizations see tasks holistically and in a cross-sectoral manner, but also that sustainability issues are considered in a geographical and cultural context. Every single geographical area has its own character—be it in terms of demography, natural resources, or industry. What is sustainable in a small city like Drammen is different from what is sustainable in the northern city of Bardu. In the latter, it might be sustainable to buy food from local producers who sell meat from free-range Angus bulls rather than to buy industrially produced meat from the Netherlands or Argentina. Free-range livestock keep the vegetation down and are outside almost all year round. They create social and environmental value in this way. In the former, it might be sustainable to buy catering services from refugees who have started their own company. Therefore, we cannot ask an expert on sustainability what is generally sustainable. Each municipality and public organization must find out and justify its decisions themselves, based on sustainability dimensions and the knowledge they have of their own municipality. In other words, sustainability is context-dependent.

Municipalities are often organized into agencies that reflect their social mission and purpose. The commercial agency is meant to stimulate local business development, while health and social agencies contribute to good living conditions for youth and care for the elderly. The environment and transport agencies are responsible for bicycle paths and roads, and so on. The districts in Oslo have organized their services according to purpose in the same way, but unlike agencies, the districts have a geographical division. They are, in addition to the city councils and heads of administration, the only unit in the municipality that has a cross-sectoral focus within a geographical area. Although the districts in Oslo are responsible for their own services, agency-oriented, and the size of large municipalities, they still have a greater eye for their own residents' needs and what goes on in the district than the municipal agencies and enterprises. Smaller municipalities, like larger ones, have agencies with sectoral tasks and expertise, but like the city districts, they often come closer to residents' wishes and needs than larger municipalities with their more bureaucratic structure. In large municipalities, there is a greater distance between the top—where decisions are made—and the bottom of the hierarchy—where frustrations are felt. In smaller municipalities, employees often sit next to each other and drop by to discuss challenges. They are also closer to the local community. This may provide a better starting point for seeing municipality issues more holistically as well as from citizens' perspectives. Such an organization can counteract silo tendencies and create better and more socially sustainable solutions. As a participant in the Work Research Institute's project on sustainable procurement of food put it:

Sometimes it's easier to get things done in a smaller municipality. There is a direct route to the management, and we have a clearer understanding of whom to approach and whom we need to persuade a bit more. In larger municipalities, they have a larger organization, and then collaboration becomes more cumbersome.

Community planning and development in municipalities is expected to move in a more sustainable direction. This involves an organization of the public sector that is more mindful to cooperation across sectors and departments. However, this conflicts with Management by Objectives and Results (MBOR) and the way in which it is practiced today. MBOR is linked to a market logic that centres around that which is quantitatively measurable and a "governance by numbers" (Supiot, 2017), which are used for controlling each sector, and promote competition between municipalities. If public enterprises had instead been managed based on systems designed for the public sector, and not on market logic and competition, holistic management and likely also sustainability would be easier to incorporate.

Organizing to ensure sustainability is, in many ways, the opposite of the current silo-dominated governance, where organizations compete on quantitative parameters based on measures of results and activities. As it stands, each public organization has its specialized tasks and goals to manage and deliver on. While some specialization is necessary in the organization of services, hyper-specialization leads to the fragmentation of organizations, which inevitably comes at the expense of holistic thinking. In particular, social sustainability typically falls between two areas—i.e., when public organizations build densely near traffic hubs, which can, in turn, make access to parks and green areas more difficult for residents. Therefore, the three sustainability dimensions must be viewed more in conjunction in community planning (Hanssen et al., 2015).

On Social Sustainability

What is the social sustainability that is often ignored? There are various definitions of social sustainability, but embedded in most of these we find concerns for social justice and economic development as well as universal and basic human rights for all, including access to sufficient resources to keep families and communities healthy and safe. This definition of social sustainability is broad, and the world is a large and diverse place. For sustainability to remain a relevant and useful tool, it is important that it is adapted to the local context. Sustainability is context-dependent, and social sustainability in Norwegian municipalities is different from social sustainability in developing countries.

Social sustainability encompasses a broad range of different aspects of people's living conditions and quality of life. This includes a safe and good place to live, educational opportunities, decent working conditions, social belonging, the absence of discrimination, and the opportunity to participate in decision-making processes that affect people's everyday lives. Sustainable development in cities and communities is important for social sustainability because our surroundings matter both for health and wellbeing. In urban development, social sustainability concerns where and what we build, and how we can create good and safe living environments. In this regard, municipalities are key players because they determine specific land use and set long-term goals for community development. Through inclusive planning processes, municipalities can facilitate user participation and the involvement of different groups, which can contribute to creating a sense of belonging. Furthermore, the municipality can plan for good living conditions and social meeting places that could improve local communities.

The concept of Municipality 3.0 has gained popularity recently and attempts to describe a future where residents are more active contributors in solving welfare challenges. Joint governance between the municipality and self-organized voluntary organizations is an old practice, but has now been rebranded and brought forward as a new ideal in public governance, motivated by the failures of NPM solutions prioritizing product and service delivery from large commercial organizations. This has not always worked well in all areas and geographical locations. Prior to NPM, public organizations already collaborated to a larger extent with NGOs and civil society organizations. In this sense, we are seeing a sort of revitalization—at least of this idea—albeit under different conditions. If we were to go by these policy statements, collaboration with civil society could again become more central in public service delivery and management.

Co-governance and co-creation can take many different forms (Reichborn-Kjennerud & Ophaug, 2018; Røiseland & Vabo, 2008). New ideals in governance often embrace ways of working that have co-creation and social innovation as starting points. However, centralized governance, organization, decision-making, and measurement, implemented within the NPM regime since the 1980s, do not align well with this way of thinking. Overall, while there is a number of different definitions, co-creation is about identifying the problem together with those concerned, then choosing or designing a solution and producing it together with them (Røiseland & Lo, 2019). However, the way these ideas are implemented in practice will affect whether the outcome is actually responsive to those concerned. It is important that co-creation is achieved without a primary focus on commercial forces. Otherwise, we end up merely facilitating new markets that, in practice, prevent co-creation. True co-creation requires that public organizations build their offers around initiatives taken by employees and residents. The question is also who has the power, money, and time to participate in all these committees set up by public organizations. In reality, it is often developers, whose initiatives can end up becoming legitimized by a few citizen representatives also sitting in some of the same meetings, but who are largely ignored. That said, co-creation implemented in a proper way still has the potential to help promote social sustainability and ensure good liveable places. However, this requires the authorities to take into account user and citizen perspectives to a far greater extent, for example, by asking what is perceived as frustrating for citizens or which sustainability initiatives residents may offer that the municipality can embrace. It may be a good idea to limit commercial solutions and cooperate to a greater extent with non-profit and voluntary organizations (Reichborn-Kjennerud & Ophaug, 2018).

Like all large organizations, public enterprises need to allocate responsibilities and tasks. In addition, the authorities must justify the way they use taxpayer money. Therefore, they set goals for spending and try to measure their results. There is, however, an apparent contradiction between the silo orientation, standardization, management by objectives and results, and thinking holistically and based on location. Also, measuring societal results is difficult and even impossible within the current framework. There is no simple quantitative indicator to which social sustainability can be reduced. In their eagerness to secure control, be good, and not discriminate, public authorities standardize their services, oversimplify, and introduce reporting regimes that require a lot of work from people who could otherwise have used this time to deliver services. To be useful, quantitative measurement must be used with caution and only where relevant. More qualitative modes of thinking and evaluating are necessary if we are to achieve the goals of social sustainability, and these need to be balanced against the quantitative (Voldnes, 2012a, 2012b).

The more fragmented public organizations become, the less they are able to see the results of their collective efforts, and their consequences and impacts. The less municipalities and public organizations are able to make an effort collectively, the worse the results become. Often, initiatives or solutions end up being neither socially nor environmentally sustainable. Despite the hyperfocus on public spending, tax money is not used for the best possible result. While measurement has its uses, it must not undermine sustainable development. Sustainability is synonymous with holistic thinking. For something to be sustainable, we must think of local solutions adapted to different places with their own challenges and contexts, while simultaneously keeping in mind the larger whole, and the impact of these solutions at the world scale. The control systems we have today, perhaps even the sustainability indicators themselves, can undermine real sustainability work. Within the field of urban and community planning, this may entail new approaches involving real co-creation with residents.

REFERENCES

Bindhulatha, S., & Kumar, A. (2021). Green Pilots–Walking Those Green Miles—A Review. *PalArch's Journal of Archaeology of Egypt/Egyptology, 18*(4), 5719–5727.

Boye, E. (2019). *Sirkulær framtid–om skiftet fra lineær til sirkulær økonomi. Framtiden i våre hender.* Rapport August 2019, 5–59. https://www.framtiden.no/filer/dokumenter/Rapporter/2019/2019-aug-sirkulaer-framtid.pdf

Hanssen, G. S., & Aarsæther, N. H. (2018). *Plan-og bygningsloven 2008: En lov for vår tid?* Universitetsforlaget.

Hanssen, G. S., Hofstad, H., & Saglie, I. L. (Eds.). (2015). *Kompakt byutvikling. Muligheter og utfordringer.* Universitetsforlaget.

Harvold, K. A. (2002). *Consensus or Conflict? Experiences with Local Agenda 21 Forums* (p. 117). NIBR. Working Paper 2002.

Hofstad, H. (2013). *Håndtering av 'wicked problems' i kommunal planlegging.* PhD Thesis. University of Oslo.

Hofstad, H. (2021). *Sosialt bærekraftige lokalsamfunn—En litteraturstudie* (p. 7). NIBR report 2021.

Kainzbauer, A., & Rungruang, P. (2019). Science Mapping the Knowledge Base on Sustainable Human Resource Management, 1982–2019. *Sustainability, 11*(14), 3938.

Kara, S. (2023). *Cobalt Red: How the Blood of the Congo Powers Our Lives.* SD Books.

Machin, D., & Liu, Y. (2023). How Tick List Sustainability Distracts from Actual Sustainable Action: The UN 2030 Agenda for Sustainable Development.

Critical Discourse Studies, 21(2), 164–181. https://doi.org/10.1108 0/17405904.2023.2197606

Mair, S., Jones, A., Ward, J., Christie, I., Druckman, A., & Lyon, F. (2018). A Critical Review of the Role of Indicators in Implementing the Sustainable Development Goals. In W. Leal Filho (Ed.), *Handbook of Sustainability Science and Research* (pp. 41–56). Springer. https://doi.org/10.1007/978-3-319-63007-6_3

McKie, R. (2021, January 3). Child labour, toxic leaks: The price we could pay for a greener future. *The Guardian*. https://www.theguardian.com/environment/2021/jan/03/child-labour-toxic-leaks-the-price-we-could-pay-for-a-greener-future

Merry, S. E. (2011). Measuring the World: Indicators, Human Rights, and Global Governance. *Current Anthropology, 52*(S3), S83–S95.

Millet, A., & Kuldova, T. Ø. (2024). Labour Migration, Crime, and 'Compliance Washing': A Tailor's Odyssey from an African Workshop to European Luxury Fashion Multinationals. In T. Ø. Kuldova, J. Østbø, & C. Shore (Eds.), *Compliance, Defiance, and 'Dirty' Luxury: New Perspectives on (Anti-) Corruption in Elite Contexts*. Palgrave Macmillan.

Piketty, T. (2014). *Capital in the twenty-first century*. Harvard University Press.

Reichborn-Kjennerud, K., & Ophaug, E. (2018). Resident Participation in an Era of Societal Self-Organisation: The Public Administrative Response in Tøyen. *Scandinavian Journal of Public Administration, 22*(2), 65–87. https://doi.org/10.58235/sjpa.v22i2.11443

Røiseland, A., & Lo, C. (2019). Samskaping–nyttig begrep for norske forskere og praktikere? *Norsk Statsvitenskapelig Tidsskrift, 35*(1), 51–58. https://doi.org/10.18261/issn.1504-2936-2019-01-03

Røiseland, A., & Vabo, S. I. (2008). Governance på norsk. Samstyring som empirisk og analytisk fenomen. *Norsk Statsvitenskapelig Tidsskrift, 24*(1–2), 86–107. https://doi.org/10.18261/ISSN1504-2936-2008-01-02-05

Supiot, A. (2017). *Governance by Numbers: The Making of a Legal Model of Allegiance*. Bloomsbury.

Telleria, J., & Garcia-Arias, J. (2022). The Fantasmatic Narrative of 'Sustainable Development.' A Political Analysis of the 2030 Global Development Agenda. *Environment and Planning C: Politics and Space, 40*(1), 241–259. https://doi.org/10.1177/23996544211018214

Voldnes, F. (2012a). Folkevalgt styring eller markedsstyring? *Samfunn og Økonomi, 2*, 6–27.

Voldnes, F. (2012b). *Markedsretting av offentlig sektor: Virkemidler og alternativer*. Fagforbundet. https://assets-global.website-files.com/65e884f8fffb6d61 0d77c46d/65fc3739f69e601b3352005b_Markedsretting%20des%20 2012.pdf.

CHAPTER 3

The Origins and Main Tools of New Public Management

Abstract Research documents that New Public Management (NPM) has added a new layer of bureaucracy and red tape to the old rule bureaucracy, a so-called hybrid solution, without improving quality. Welfare services often appear as fragmented and system loyal rather than centred around the needs of employees and users of public services. This culminated in the demand for a trust-reform in Norway. This chapter describes the gradual introduction of NPM measures, including the fragmentation of public organizations, the use of competition, incentives, contractual methods, reporting, and documentation. This has led to less trust in employees, less real accountability, risk aversion, and less room for professional discretion. Complex societal results are seldom possible to trace back to measures from isolated public organizations. Therefore, NPM overestimates what is feasible to measure, promises more than it can deliver, and costs more than assumed.

Keywords New public management • Management by objectives and results • Norway • Scientific management

What is New Public Management (NPM) and how did this phenomenon arise? NPM is a broad but useful umbrella term that refers to the

© The Author(s), under exclusive license to Springer Nature Switzerland AG 2025
K. Reichborn-Kjennerud, *Sustainable Urban Transitions and New Public Management*,
https://doi.org/10.1007/978-3-031-82307-7_3

administrative doctrines that have dominated the reform agenda in many OECD[1] countries since the 1970s (Hood, 1991). Christopher Hood began using the term in 1991 to describe the way public authorities had begun to emulate management and leadership in the private sector (Hood, 1991). According to him, NPM—a collection of reform measures, such as Management by Objectives and Results (MBOR), key performance indicators (KPI), public enterprises, contract management, and more—was inspired by reforms implemented by Margaret Thatcher and Ronald Reagan in the UK and the US towards the end of the 1980s. However, which systems and reform measures actually fall under the umbrella term NPM often remains unclear, as there are many different models and variants.

In line with the international trend that NPM represents, Norway introduced reforms, from the 1980s onwards, to make the public sector more efficient. The basis for the reform measures in Norway was laid out in a report titled *En bedre organisert stat*[2] (A Better Organized State) by the Consumer and Administration Department in 1989, and the Hermansen Committee. Measures—which can be termed as NPM, or marketization of the state—were gradually introduced with the Gro Harlem Brundtland government's renewal program in the 1980s and continued by the conservative government led by Kåre Willoch. These measures have profoundly changed the way the Norwegian public sector operates. Today, the main emphasis is on efficiency and goal achievement, on competition within public organizations and between public and private enterprises, and on incentive systems for public employees. Public organizations have been transformed into companies and divided into smaller parts (Christensen & Lægreid, 2022).

NPM is not a unified reform. Rather, the phenomenon is described as a series of different measures introduced over time. Taken together, they can be characterized as a set of doctrines, including stronger control of professions, more standards, more quantitative goals for performance,

---

[1] The Organization for Economic Cooperation and Development. The OECD is an intergovernmental organization founded in 1961 to advice governments on how to deliver better policies.

[2] NOU 1989, 5. https://www.regjeringen.no/globalassets/upload/kilde/odn/tmp/2002/0034/ddd/pdfv/154719-nou1989-5.pdf

more control of results rather than process, more frugal resource use and management, and more competition within the public sector (Hood, 1991). The defenders of these reforms argue that the measures have been misunderstood and not always implemented in accordance with intentions (Bekkelund, 2018). They also believe that many of the reforms have been better than their reputation suggests and have actually solved some important challenges. Critics on the other hand, believe that these reforms have led to increased micro-management, bureaucratization, and more control (Linder et al., 2018).

Tormod Hermansen, the former head of the Ministry of Finance and of the state-owned telecommunications company Telenor, was central in the introduction of NPM reforms in Norway and led the influential Hermansen Committee. In a debate article, he assessed how well these reforms have worked, describing how their actual development has followed six main tracks: market-based organizational and management forms, purchaser-provider split, contracts, quasi-contracts, and executive pay incentives to facilitate competition, privatization and partial privatization, more independent state agencies, such as supervisory bodies, and more emphasis placed on individual rights under the law. The state introduced MBOR, which was supposed to give more room for action than the previous activity-based budget and rule-based governance. The Ministries also delegated more operational tasks to subordinate bodies. The driving forces behind these changes have been internationalization, individualization, and liberal ideology (Hermansen, 2013).

The changes have been extensive, both in their breadth and depth, and spanned over many years, resulting in a state where hybrid organizational forms have grown with an increasing number of layers of control and management (Engelstad & Steen-Johnsen, 2010; Christensen & Lægreid, 2017). Privatization and deregulation have replaced the social democratic and active state with a regulatory state. This regulation costs taxpayers and consumers money because someone has to pay for the state's and agencies' (as well as businesses') expenses of complying with the rules set by the regulatory state. These changes have resulted in a series of unintended consequences. Focus has shifted to control, reporting, details, breaches, and legality testing, and the result has been a growing bureaucracy (Veggeland, 2009, 2010). This regulatory state privileges large companies, whose legal teams can ensure compliance with these ever-growing regulations, over smaller actors who do not have the same legal and administrative capacity. In other words, this form of regulation favors big capital.

The focus on control is intensified by media revelations of individual cases, as scandals often lead to more regulations and further compliance requirements, fuelling the growth of the audit, consulting, and tech industries, or the "compliance-industrial complex" (Kuldova, 2022). Moreover, the Office of the Auditor General's (OAG) compliance audits can also lead to ministries and subordinate agencies becoming even more detail-oriented. That said, some of their performance audit reports are of high quality, much needed, and often critical. As a response to criticism, leaders in the public sector can often implement further detailed measures and prioritize policy communication demonstrating that they are not making mistakes. While responses to these audits could take the form of holistic and long-term solutions, in practice, we see more short-term measures designed to avoid criticism.

According to Hermansen, the state has not necessarily become better organized with NPM, but differently organized and managed. He claims that some implemented measures have been necessary, but he also believes that the current organization does not provide incentives for public organizations to improve and prevents the use of competence in the organization for generating best possible solutions (Hermansen, 2013).

In NPM and agency theory, both the principal and the agents are motivated by self-interest. To ensure good results, the principal (i.e., the one who delegates money) must therefore control the agent (i.e., the one who performs tasks). These measures, designed to maintain control, result in red tape or administrative tasks, such as reporting and documentation requirements, contracts administration and follow-up, external control through the OAG and municipal audits, and internal control. Compliance audits can create a need for more internal administrative control as management in companies must document that they are doing something to correct identified deviations (Reichborn-Kjennerud, 2013, 2014a, 2014b, 2015a, 2015b, 2021). This control is also often reinforced further down the organizational hierarchy in the form of so-called "over-implementation" (Linder et al., 2018).

At the same time, public authorities' control increasingly takes the form of governance (Van den Dool et al., 2015), which involves the formal and informal cooperation between public organizations, market actors, and civil society to solve complex tasks and societal challenges (Røiseland & Vabo, 2008). This means that public organizations increasingly enter into contracts between public organizations, and public and private organizations. Governance is assumed by its proponents to provide more room for co-creation with citizens than the old forms of public administration. However, researchers still debate what genuine co-creation actually involves, and have not yet found any definitive answer (Røiseland, 2023). As of now, the concept appears as a buzzword and as ideologically driven, while the content and practice is arbitrary. Still, if developers do not invite residents to participate in important decisions, but only open for comments on the less important details during the implementation phase, it can hardly be understood as genuine co-creation (Bentzen, 2021). However, the problem with governance theory is that it does not take into account that there may be conflicting interests and power imbalances. Instead, it is built on the underlying assumption that if everyone participates, then harmony and consensus result spontaneously, while real conflicts of interest and problems disappear. In such multistakeholder governance, power imbalances, conflicts of interests, and antagonisms are glossed over, disavowed, or suppressed (Kuldova, 2024).

An important question to ask is how democracy is affected by these governance systems (Van den Dool et al., 2015). Real democracy involves representation and actual influence by those affected by decisions. Without a real possibility of influencing decisions, the participants only end up legitimizing the decisions of those in power. Real co-creation would mean that participants have a real opportunity to contribute in cases and decisions that impact them and risk undermining their interests. At the same time, we find, in practice, conflicts between the efficient and timely execution of policies and attempts to ensure the democratic nature of processes through broad involvement. There are many pitfalls. For instance, for the sake of simplicity, decision-makers may involve the most resourceful organized interest groups simply because it takes less time. Typically, it is the resourceful and those with business interests who have the time, money, and manpower to engage in these participation processes, influence outcomes, and safeguard their interests. Therefore, the actual ways in which democracy is implemented become important. According to Van den Dool, the organization, systems, and the way governance is exercised in cities should be evaluated in practice to see if and how they contribute to real democracy (Van den Dool et al., 2015).

Key Aspects of NPM in Theory and Practice

As already mentioned, reform measures were introduced in Norway starting in the 1970s to make the operation of the public sector more akin to the private sector, focusing on competition, MBOR, and cost control. The idea was to keep politicians at arm's length from the implementation of policy. Quality was to be assured and costs reduced by outsourcing the work of public employees, stimulating competition between employees, and insisting on quantified assessments of what employees do. Politicians would then simply order the policies, and subordinate public organizations would carry out the required tasks. Such orders were implemented through contracts or contract-like documents down through the state and municipal hierarchies, such as the Ministries' letters of allocation and order documents for procurement of home care services. Many and varied, reforms in Norway over the past decades can be characterized—if following Hood's interpretation (1991)—as part of this NPM phenomenon. Everything from the enterprise model in specialist health services, including activity-based financing, MBOR in the educational sector, competitive tendering of nursing homes, opening up publicly-funded private kindergartens, and partial privatization of the former state-owned telecommunication company, to the transformation of the energy industry can be described as NPM tools (Bekkelund, 2018). These tools were chosen by the Ministries themselves as the most efficient governance mechanism.

Internationally, the development of NPM can be traced back to the neoliberal ideological trends in English-speaking countries. What was new in New Public Management was the market orientation, which stood in contrast to the Old Public Management (OPM), where the state was managed hierarchically. While under NPM the state is still controlled hierarchically, with the marketization of the state there are now more control layers on top of the old ones (Lægreid, 2017). NPM reforms were meant to increase efficiency in the production of public services. MBOR was another reform introduced in the 1960s and 1970s to shift focus from input factors to the effects of spending. Both MBOR and NPM tools were gradually introduced through a series of reforms.

Key features of these NPM reforms include the organization in result units, internal pricing, the use of unit price financing, incentive schemes, reward mechanisms, competitive tendering, and privatization. These control mechanisms, in addition to MBOR, are enshrined in Norwegian financial regulations. There has been little research on the results and unintended consequences of these reforms, but studies carried out cannot document that NPM reforms have cut costs or produced better results. In the UK, research finds the opposite: the government costs more and produces poorer results with an NPM organization (Hood & Dixon, 2015; Lægreid, 2017). This is due in part to the practice of services being purchased rather than the work done internally in state organizations. The number of public employees in the UK has been reduced but the total cost has not when purchases are taken into account. The quality of services, on the other hand, has gone down. There are more complaints and rising dissatisfaction with public services (Hood & Dixon, 2015; Torfing, 2016).

How well NPM reforms work depends on the local context and can turn out more or less well. Result indicators provide far too limited information about the consequences of these management forms and do not take into account values like participation, democracy, professional discretion, equality before the law, responsiveness to citizens, and politicians' ability to govern (Christensen & Lægreid, 2004). NPM reforms were originally intended to make it easier for leaders in public organizations to be held accountable, but broader assessments than performance indicators are needed to ensure the accountability of administration and politicians for the use of taxpayer money. When responsibility is distributed and delegated across so many levels and between different organizational units and suppliers, the end result can be the evasion of responsibility. NPM organization is also poorly suited to handle complex problems, such as climate or societal security challenges, where public enterprises must work across sectors and cooperate (Christensen & Lægreid, 2022). A central question is therefore whether we should organize and govern the state differently to mobilize employees and citizens' resources in the renewal of the public sector (Hood & Dixon, 2015; Torfing, 2016).

Competitive tenders and unit price financing are two of the most important measures in the restructuring of the Norwegian welfare state (Innset, 2020). These organizational forms have been introduced in elderly care, child welfare, home services, specialist health services, schools, education, research, and more. For example, hospitals have been organized as enterprises: they receive parts of their financing through unit price financing based on patients' diagnosis (DRG system). The school system has been standardized, becoming goal- and results-driven.

This type of organization requires interaction through contracts, which are assumed to contribute to better control of what the state enterprises are doing. The need for increased control stems from the underlying economic organization theory behind NPM. It recommends the use of contract management and centralization, while prescribing decentralization. In the introduction of NPM tools, these two concerns must be balanced. If accountability is most emphasized, strict hierarchical control becomes the result (Christensen & Lægreid, 2022). If efficiency is emphasized, the hierarchy is more dissolved and underlying enterprises, employees, and partners get more room for discretion. When control is centralized, activities in underlying organizations must be followed up with performance measurement to check that agreements are adhered to.

Ideally, NPM should measure societal results, but this is difficult in practice because there is not a one-to-one relationship between what a public organization does and how children, young people, the elderly, or adult workers fare in society and in the labor market. Social development is a result of a conglomerate of many complex factors, where a myriad of different systems and actions interact. When public organizations are held accountable based on simple metrics for activities counted and interpreted as results simply because that is what is possible to measure, it does not yield good sustainable results in a holistic sense (Bianchi, 2015).

The NPM system encourages the production of many units of something that can be counted. At the same time, even in economic theory, it is clear that the public sector should take care of precisely those tasks and social goods that are unsuitable to be traded on a market, and which therefore cannot be counted or traded as mere services or products. It is also the public sector's task to safeguard the commons. Public responsibilities are typically investments and tasks that a private actor would not find profitable, but which nevertheless have great social value. Examples of things that should be ensured collectively are roads, parks, clean air, access to nature, clean water, education, health, and so forth. Some of these benefits often have a greater value than is possible to put a price tag on. However, NPM is not a system rigged to see or consider the commons and community values. It is rather organized around standardization, management, and control of top-down and organization-specific goals. Goals are set from the top and operationalized by subordinate levels, and should preferably be measurable and quantitative. In this measurement, the attention is thus directed towards relatively simple measures and causal relationships. The commons that can contribute in complex ways to good results, if these arenas work as expected, often require an interplay of forces and cannot be measured as easily. The measurement system therefore conflicts with the sustainability agenda, which entails thinking more holistically and in a cross-sectoral manner. This means thinking locally and in a context-dependent way. In this type of perspective, municipalities and state organizations could identify what sustainability means for them locally and weigh environmental, social, and economic considerations in their particular cultural, geographical, and social context by using discretionary judgement. Such a system of governance would also require more trust in employees.

As previously mentioned, centralization is a key feature of NPM. It entails solving similar tasks in similar ways to save time and to ensure control over what is being delivered. Previously, different public services for different groups of the population were managed and organized in unique ways. We had schools, kindergartens, and hospitals organized around their specific and unique functions and social mission. With NPM, these have become seen and managed as interchangeable organizations with result units. Managing a hospital is assumed to be the same as managing a university. As a result, we now talk about enterprises and organizations instead of schools and hospitals. These organizations interact in a pseudo-market with contracts, unit price financing, benchmarking, and incentive schemes. Internally, public enterprises are run like businesses with communication departments, the outsourcing of services, internal pricing and invoicing, the division of responsibility, and measurement of results.

Procurement is often centralized through long-lasting and large framework contracts that cannot necessarily be terminated just because politicians with different agendas come to power (Innset, 2020). If public organizations wish to opt out of contracts, it costs money and often has dire consequences. The contract period is set, the products and services to be delivered are agreed upon for a specific price over a certain period of time, and changes inevitably incur extra costs. This contractualization sets very concrete limits to what is possible and makes it hard to reimagine governance in practice. Furthermore, this organization of the public sector around procurement and contracts deprives elected politicians of power because it is the contracts that set the limits for what is ultimately possible to decide. However, politicians have also actively given up power precisely by converting agencies into public enterprises. Representatives for the Ministries sit on the board of these enterprises and the only way politicians can influence the way the company is run is by overthrowing the board. The aforementioned report *A Better Organized State* (NOU

1989, 5)[3] by the Hermansen Committee laid the foundation for the establishment of such state enterprises within energy, telecommunications, and transport. For example, as of January 1, 1995, Televerket changed its name to Telenor and the former leader, Tormod Hermansen, became its CEO. Statkraft, Statnett, Jernbaneverket, and Vy (formerly NSB) were converted into companies in the same way.

With the transformation of public agencies into businesses, public organizations have become more focused on marketing. The job of communication departments is to tell the outside world and taxpayers that the public enterprise is doing well—often despite citizens' experiences to the contrary. The communication and Public Relations (PR) staff in the Norwegian public is increasing, as does the use of consultants and external PR experts. At the same time, tasks are, to a lesser extent, solved internally in public organizations. Instead of building core competence internally, tasks are put out to tender (Hermansen, 2013).

Even though a goal of state reform through NPM was democratization, the introduced market techniques mean that politicians' power has decreased. In this way, NPM stands in conflict with democratic governance logic (Christensen & Lægreid, 2004). Public organizations have less competence in-house and have to purchase both the actual and consulting services, thus becoming ever more dependent on the market and on solutions offered on the market, which may not necessarily be the best solutions from the point of view of sustainability.

Why is thinking critically about NPM and contemporary governance, audit, and accounting so important? Accounting practices profoundly shape how we perceive, understand, and seek to shape reality. The epistemologies embedded in and underpinning these managerial techniques shape our societies in profound ways. They have, in other words, significant "epistemic power" (Kuldova & Nordrik, 2023). Many public organizations have started to use business accounting instead of cash accounting, which allows elected politicians to see what the funds are used for, as opposed to business accounting that follows a logic of profit. When business-oriented accounts are used, it means that the traditional budget as a management tool disappears and is replaced with financial performance management. Again, politicians come to have less control over the administrative leaders of enterprises. Business-oriented accounting also

---

[3] https://www.regjeringen.no/globalassets/upload/kilde/odn/tmp/2002/0034/ddd/pdfv/154719-nou1989-5.pdf

means that public services appear expensive, further facilitating privatization (Voldnes, 2012a, 2012b). Therefore, there are fewer opportunities to make decisions about the strategy and operation of public organizations, and these are also harder to identify (Innset, 2020).

The operation of the public sector should be based on laws passed in the Norwegian Parliament (The Storting), and not by market principles. In this sense, the OPM was better aligned with democratic values than the NPM, which does not distinguish between private and public sectors, and wherein power is transferred to the market. This system thus undermines democratic governance and values (Box et al., 2001). The only thing politicians can do in this new system is to give signals through so-called letters of allocation with conditions linked to them (Innset, 2020). However, the administration in state and municipal organizations, and leaders of large agencies and state companies acquire more power in this system (Innset, 2020). The balance of power therefore shifts to the executive branch, at the expense of the legislative—i.e., from politics to administrative management. Budget balance and cost control come to guide politics and political decisions. In the process, management of the government as a business compromises fundamental values, such as legality, representative government, individual freedom, and the separation of powers.

The classic traditional model of governing the state—OPM—originated from Germany and Max Weber's principles for an efficient bureaucracy. In his theory of the bureaucracy, Weber emphasized accountability from top to bottom in a hierarchy. Politicians decide from the top and subordinate organizations implement the policy. Each leader and worker reports to a superior, and is held accountable by that person. The control system's principles are rational and law-based. The bureaucratic system is governed by a set of rules and regulations that originate from the law, and the bureaucrat's role is subordinate to the political. According to this theory, civil servants should conscientiously implement what the superior authorities have instructed. Ideally, the administration should be completely separated from political issues, even though administrative employees can often influence policy formation in practice. With NPM, however, power is moved away from politicians to the administration and executive branch. The idea is that politicians should steer, while the administration should row. This affords a larger scope for the administration, albeit fewer opportunities for democratic control for citizens (Christensen & Lægreid, 2004).

Compared to charismatic and traditional forms of governance, Weber's bureaucracy was superior. Advocates for the renewal of the public sector in the 1970s and 1980s, however, compared bureaucracy with the market and thought that the way the bureaucracy worked was too cumbersome. They wanted to organize the state more according to market principles. According to the market model, the idea of reforming the public sector was to decentralize the administration and management of state organizations and delegate so that subordinate units could make discretionary assessments. Management through contracts, competition with emphasis on customer service, and the measurement of results were part and parcel of the model. The measurement of results was meant to replace rule-based control. More freedom was to be given to managers so that they could use their own judgment and professional discretion, while simultaneously being held accountable for results. Privatization of public enterprises, where the Ministries in some cases held a majority of stocks, was also part of this package, such as in the aforementioned cases of the conversion of agencies into telephone and oil companies, and the privatization of post offices, and air transport. Ideally, under the NPM system, we should have seen more internal participation, flexibility, and deregulation in public organizations. However, in practice, we saw a hybrid variant of the old bureaucracy, which supports the market solutions, in turn generating more administrative work (Christensen & Lægreid, 2004).

The NPM solutions we have today are made possible by the traditional bureaucracy—OPM—which, in its time, paved the way for the industrial revolution and a modern economy. NPM has been seen as modernization, and has mutated and been given new nicknames over time, such as network governance, lean management, or trust-based management (Lapsley & Miller, 2024), while boiling down to the same foundational principles. Frederick Taylor's *Principles of Scientific Management* (1919) brought forth the solutions that became the precursor to automation, industrialization, and modern markets. Taylor famously conducted time and motion studies on workers to see how work could be carried out as efficiently as possible under strict control. In the long run, the idea was that machines would replace humans. Today, researchers are discussing whether the new digital control and algorithmic governance in society resembles Taylorism, only adapted for the age of surveillance capitalism (Zuboff, 2019; Skorstad, 2003; Taylor, 1919).

The modernization of the Norwegian public sector since the 1980s has thus come at the expense of cooperation and can also create unintended consequences, such as increased costs and lower quality. Moreover, measures taken by one public organization can block and undermine measures taken by others. Together, these measures therefore do not necessarily create the promised societal benefits.

The Effects of New Public Management

An increasing number of people fall out of the labor market, despite policies wanting everyone to work.[4] Norway ranks at the top in Europe, with 10.6% of the population on disability benefits in 2023.[5] There are indications that not everything is functioning optimally within the school and health systems, and in work organizations. International comparisons show that early school dropout is relatively common in Norway (Steffensen, 2016).

A main change NPM led to was steering public organizations towards focusing on activities (output) produced rather than on resources put into the system. The rates of throughput of students and patients are the main focus for Norwegian universities and hospitals, and have been an important goal in Norwegian education and health policy.[6] It is nevertheless ideally results (outcome), or the societal improvement that the state organization has contributed to, that is the most interesting information, such as better health, increased national security, justice, etc.

For the system to work effectively, it becomes important to choose the right measurement indicators that actually contribute to socially sustainable results. At the same time, societal results are very challenging to measure and even more difficult to link to a government-funded program. Herein lies the major challenge for NPM. It works as intended when the government buys goods and services that can easily be counted. The more

---

[4] "Flere i arbeid," Meld. St. 46 (2012–2013). https://www.regjeringen.no/no/dokumenter/meld-st-46-20122013/id733259/sec3

[5] https://www.ssb.no/sosiale-forhold-og-kriminalitet/trygd-og-stonad/statistikk/uforetrygdede

[6] For example, see "Aktivitet, liggetid og gjennomstrømning i somatiske sykehus 2016" (Activity, length of stay and throughput in somatic hospitals 2016). https://www.helsedirektoratet.no/statistikk/samdata-spesialisthelsetjenesten/analysenotater-samdata-spesialisthelsetjenesten/02-2017%20Aktivitetsniv%C3%A5%20i%20somatiske%20sykehus.pdf/_/attachment/inline/141bb3d3-8030-4945-aab1-fd041f823645:d477eba8b4af02c778998aaf026046ea830d8636/02-2017%20Aktivitetsniv%C3%A5%20i%20somatiske%20sykehus.pdf

the activity resembles goods and services in the private sector, the better the system works because it is then easier to create meaningful result indicators. Social welfare and analytical services, such as research, are more difficult to quantify and create indicators for, as more unique and complex tasks require expertise to assess quality and cannot be standardized easily.

There are indications that NPM leads to more people being left out of the labor market, a reduction in free arenas and meeting places, and greater inequalities in society, with consequences for public health. This development is difficult to isolate, identify, and link to the market-mimicking systems in the state. The cost of planning and designing contracts, contract management, and the measurement of results is not included in the assessment of whether NPM is cost-effective as a system. The perception of NPM as efficient and cost-saving is therefore typically exaggerated.

In this chapter, we have seen how Norwegian authorities took a number of measures from the 1980s onwards to get more out of taxpayer money. The chapter has questioned whether we have actually gotten more out of taxpayer money, or whether these reforms have had additional costs—economic, social, and for our democracy. In the next chapter, we will further substantiate these concerns by looking at different sectors in practice.

REFERENCES

Bekkelund, A. S. (2018). Et forsvar for New Public Management. *Stat & Styring*, 28(2), 2–6. https://doi.org/10.18261/ISSN0809-750X-2018-02-02

Bentzen, T. Ø. (2021). Samskabt styring: Potentialer og udfordringer. *Politica*, 53(3), 261–279. https://doi.org/10.7146/politica.v53i3.130456

Bianchi, C. (2015). Enhancing Joined-Up Government and Outcome-Based Performance Management through System Dynamics Modelling to Deal with Wicked Problems: The Case of Societal Ageing. *Systems Research and Behavioral Science*, 32(4), 502–505. https://doi.org/10.1002/sres.2341

Box, R. C., Marshall, G. S., Reed, B. J., & Reed, C. M. (2001). New Public Management and Substantive Democracy. *Public Administration Review*, 61(5), 608–619. https://doi.org/10.1111/0033-3352.00131

Christensen, T., & Lægreid, P. (2004). Governmental Autonomisation and Control: The Norwegian Way. *Public Administration and Development: The International Journal of Management Research and Practice*, 24(2), 129–135. https://doi.org/10.1002/pad.318

Christensen, T., & Lægreid, P. (2017). *Transcending New Public Management*. Routledge.

Christensen, T., & Lægreid, P. (2022). Taking Stock: New Public Management (NPM) and Post-NPM Reforms-Trends and Challenges. In A. Ladner & F. Sager (Eds.), *Handbook on the Politics of Public Administration* (pp. 38–49). https://doi.org/10.4337/9781839109447.00010

Engelstad, F., & Steen-Johnsen, K. (2010). Hva er det med hybride organisasjoner? *Nordiske Organisasjonsstudier, 12*(3), 3–8.

Hermansen, T. (2013). Ble det en bedre stat? *Stat & Styring, 23*(2), 24–25. https://doi.org/10.18261/ISSN0809-750X-2013-02-10

Hood, C. (1991). A Public Management for All Seasons? *Public Administration, 69*(1), 3–19. https://doi.org/10.1111/j.1467-9299.1991.tb00779.x

Hood, C., & Dixon, R. (2015). *A Government that Worked Better and Cost Less? Evaluating Three Decades of Reform and Change in UK Central Government.* Oxford University Press. https://doi.org/10.1093/acprof:oso/9780199687022.001.0001

Innset, O. (2020). *Markedsvendingen: Nyliberalismens historie i Norge.* Fagbokforlaget.

Kuldova, T. Ø. (2022). *Compliance-Industrial Complex: The Operating System of a Pre-Crime Society.* Palgrave Pivot. https://doi.org/10.1007/978-3-031-19224-1

Kuldova, T. Ø. (2024). Philanthrocapitalism and the Compliance-Industrial Complex: Doing 'Good', Fighting Crime, and Foreclosing Alternatives. In T. Ø. Kuldova, J. Østbø, & C. Shore (Eds.), *Compliance, Defiance and 'Dirty' Luxury: New Perspectives on Anti-Corruption in Elite Contexts.* Palgrave Macmillan.

Kuldova, T. Ø., & Nordrik, B. (2023). Workplace Investigations, the Epistemic Power of Managerialism, and the Hollowing Out of the Norwegian Model of Co-determination. *Class and Capital.* https://doi.org/10.1177/03098168231179971

Lapsley, I., & Miller, P. (Eds.). (2024). *The resilience of new public management.* Oxford University Press.

Lægreid, P. (2017). New Public Management. In *Oxford Research Encyclopedia of Politics.* https://doi.org/10.1093/acrefore/9780190228637.013.159

Linder, J., Voxted, S., Østergaard, M., Michelsen, J., Michelsen, E. B., Schloss, J., Thykjær, C., Sløk, C., Ejler, N., Langenge, M. M., & Linder, A. (2018). *New Public Management i Danmark-baggrund, erfaringer, fremtid.* Dafolo.

Reichborn-Kjennerud, K. (2013). Political Accountability and Performance Audit: The Case of the Auditor General in Norway. *Public Administration, 91*(3), 680–695. https://doi.org/10.1111/padm.12025

Reichborn-Kjennerud, K. (2014a). Auditee Strategies: An Investigation of Auditees' Reactions to the Norwegian State Audit Institution's Performance Audits. *International Journal of Public Administration, 37*(10), 685–694. https://doi.org/10.1080/01900692.2014.907309

Reichborn-Kjennerud, K. (2014b). Performance Audit and the Importance of the Public Debate. *Evaluation, 20*(3), 368–385. https://doi.org/10.1177/1356389014539869

Reichborn-Kjennerud, K. (2015a). Riksrevisjonen og tidstyvene. *Norsk Statsvitenskapelig Tidsskrift, 31*(4), 379–384. https://doi.org/10.18261/ISSN1504-2936-2015-04-08

Reichborn-Kjennerud, K. (2015b). Resistance to Control—Norwegian Ministries' and Agencies' Reactions to Performance Audit. *Public Organization Review, 15*(1), 17–32. https://doi.org/10.1007/s11115-013-0247-6

Reichborn-Kjennerud, K. (2021). Key Insights into What Makes Public Organizations Learn from Training Programs. *Nordic Journal of Working Life Studies, 12*(2), 49–66. https://doi.org/10.18291/njwls.129052

Røiseland, A. (2023). For All Seasons? Exploring the Policy-Context for Co-creation. *Public Money and Management, 44*(6), 491–499. https://doi.org/10.1080/09540962.2023.2206046

Røiseland, A., & Vabo, S. I. (2008). Governance på norsk. Samstyring som empirisk og analytisk fenomen. *Norsk Statsvitenskapelig Tidsskrift, 24*(1–2), 86–107. https://doi.org/10.18261/ISSN1504-2936-2008-01-02-05

Skorstad, E. (2003). Utviklingstrender i norsk arbeidsliv–Mot en tekniskøkonomisk idealtilstand. *I Åke Sandberg (red.), Ledning för alla*, 334–350.

Steffensen, K. (2016). Norge bedre enn EU-snittet på fem av åtte utdanningsmål. *Samfunnsspeilet, 2*, 19–25.

Taylor, F. W. (1919). *The principles of scientific management.* Harper & brothers.

Torfing, J. (2016, January 20). New Public Management har fejlet. *Videnskab DK.* https://videnskab.dk/kultur-samfund/ny-bog-new-public-management-har-fejlet/

Van den Dool, L., Hendriks, F., Gianoli, A., & Schaap, L. (2015). *The Quest for Good Urban Governance: Theoretical Reflections and International Practices.* Springer. https://doi.org/10.1007/978-3-658-10079-7

Veggeland, N. (2009). *Taming the Regulatory State: Politics and Ethics.* Edward Elgar Publishing Ltd. https://doi.org/10.4337/9781848447509

Veggeland, N. (2010). *Den nye reguleringsstaten: Idébrytinger og styringskonflikter.* Gyldendal Akademisk.

Voldnes, F. (2012a). *Markedsretting av offentlig sektor. Virkemidler og alternativer.* Fagforbundet. https://assets-global.website-files.com/65e884f8fffb6d610d77c46d/65fc3739f69e601b3352005b_Markedsretting%20des%202012.pdf

Voldnes, F. (2012b). Folkevalgt styring eller markedsstyring? *Fagbladet Samfunn og Økonomi, 2*, 6–27.

Zuboff, S. (2019). *The Age of Surveillance Capitalism: The Fight for a Human Future at the New Frontier of Power.* Profile Books.

CHAPTER 4

New Public Management in Education, Working Life, and Public Procurement

Abstract New Public Management (NPM) control systems are seductive because they appear to be so simple. The theory provides an understandable explanation of how results can be achieved and offers an opportunity to maintain control. At the same time, this need for control is at the core of the problem. Standardization, benchmarking, reporting, and organizing for competition are some central features of NPM. This chapter describes how this way of organizing can have unintended consequences that are not always positive. The need for control, embedded in NPM, often reduces the leeway of employees and gives them less possibility to adapt to the needs of people that receive their services. Control procedures take up a lot of time that could otherwise have been used to help people. Examples are given from education, research, working life, and public procurement.

Keywords New public management • Education • Public procurement • Working life

Few authors have assessed the transaction costs of NPM's competition-oriented organization of the state against what this organization actually accomplishes (Hood & Dixon, 2015). Alas, the fundamental question is whether organizing the administrative work around outsourcing and internal competition actually leads to better public goods and services. Another is whether we get a more rigid service provision and higher costs as a result of more administrative work and regulation. This is a relevant question to ask in all policy areas. This chapter discusses how the system works in practice in different policy areas, focusing mostly on education and working life, two areas most of us can relate to, are fundamental to any society, and should be at the core of its well-being.

There is a shift, both in school and working life, away from conceptions of communal responsibility towards individual responsibility. We tend to increasingly shy away from a structural analysis and prefer to use individual-oriented explanations for social ills. This depoliticized therapeutic culture characterizes contemporary Western societies. We all become our own results unit, either as a student, patient, user of welfare services, or as an employee. The pupil and student should learn to master their own life. Life mastery is introduced into the curriculum, while social responsibility and reflexivity around the organization of society are pushed into the background (Amundsen, 2022; Madsen, 2020). Focusing primarily on the individual, achievements, and competition can, however, come at the expense of well-being and have negative consequences that are not socially sustainable in the long run.

The School and the Production of Useful Individuals

The school, which prepares children and young people for the modern working life, has become increasingly standardized and oriented towards measuring student achievement. Rather paradoxically, there is thus far less room to adapt teaching according to students' strengths and weaknesses. Everyone must go through a school curriculum where skills are measured through standardized national tests. This is a policy that Norway has adopted, following OECD recommendations (Nordkvelle & Nyhus, 2017). The PISA survey showed that Norway performed worse than other OECD countries. The results from this survey stirred an atmosphere of crisis in Norwegian public life. Consequently, Kristin Clemet, who became the Minister of Education in 2001, established a quality committee to streamline the control and measurement of results in schools (Innset, 2020). Similar reforms have been implemented in the United States. George

Bush's *No child left behind* policy was implemented between 2002 and 2015. The law holds schools accountable for children's results through new national key indicators added to measurements that had already been implemented locally.

Management by Objectives and Results (MBOR) in schools is goal-oriented, thus revolving around external motivation, which can negatively affect students' sense of achievement and motivation (Ryan & Deci, 2000), and does not necessarily contribute to students' enjoyment of school. There are many theories about what prevents dropout in schools and what contributes to mastery and motivation, including the theory of the growth mindset. Research shows that children who worry about scoring poorly on tests or not reaching their goals succeed less often. Goal orientation can strengthen motivation driven by external factors, but is a less effective form of motivation. Internal motivation, on the other hand, driven by curiosity and where tasks are perceived as exciting and challenging, contributes to the joy of learning. This means that children can learn more and better, and enjoy school to a greater extent. Different children also have different strengths and weaknesses, but when everyone is measured according to the same standards, it can turn out poorly for some (Claro et al., 2016).

The dropout rate in schools has remained more or less stable since the Norwegian school reform in 1994 (Reegård & Rogstad, 2016). At the same time, society has become more complex and requires people to have more formalized rather than experience-based backgrounds. The labor market has changed, and jobs that previously did not require education now have increased professional and educational competence requirements (Reegård & Rogstad, 2016). This can exclude those who struggle with theoretical schooling. Symptomatic of these developments is the increasing proportion of girls besieged by eating disorders, increasingly younger children and youth with mental health issues, and an increasing number of boys and men doing poorly in school and at work.[1]

---

[1] See, for instance, https://forskersonen.no/kjonn-og-samfunn-kronikk-likestilling/det-bor-vekke-bekymring-at-gutter-gjor-det-darligere-enn-jenter-i-skolen/1820638, and https://www.dagensmedisin.no/artikler/2022/07/15/kraftig-okning-i-spiseforstyrrelser%2D%2Det-folkehelseproblem/

Negative Consequences for Participation, Well-Being, Motivation, and Quality in Services

Public organizations, such as employment services, the police, and health trusts are increasingly managed, standardized, and controlled. There is a tendency for less participation, increased demands for loyalty from employees, more individualization, and less influence for trade unions. Management and control of employees in public organizations is stronger than in all parts of the private sector, being strongest in health trusts and in state-owned joint-stock companies. The development accelerated from the 1990s and was reinforced after the financial crisis in 2008. Management and leadership then also took a turn towards cost control in particular, and towards preventing negative publicity of organizations and their leadership (Falkum, 2020). This tendency towards stronger management and control is something that employees in public organizations find increasingly uncomfortable. This discomfort can be illustrated with a statement from one of my informants, a former employee at the Norwegian Food Safety Authority who described her experience where she had tried to report a practice she considered unsafe following the implementation of new NPM inspired routines:

> The Ministry of Agriculture and Food ordered a full investigation of the Food Safety Authority in 2019. The report from KPMG pointed out many deficiencies. In an attempt to correct these deficiencies, the Food Safety Authority has introduced new internal routines. However, the Food Safety Authority no longer has resources for routine inspections to follow up on animal welfare. The Food Safety Authority's definition of chronically poor animal husbandry in recent years has been changed so that many serious deviations no longer appear on the list of risk animal husbandry. By changing the definition, the development looks fine. This reduced authority of the Animal Welfare Boards has resulted in a significantly reduced inspection capacity in many departments of the Food Safety Authority.
>
> The Food Safety Authority has established control teams to quality assure inspection reports. The quality assurance must be read by up to four employees before it is sent out. Many employees spend a lot of time checking reports, and there is little time to conduct inspections. The inspectors should write large parts of the report on their mobile phone, during the inspection, and send an inspection receipt to the animal owner before leaving the farm. This is very time-consuming and has given the inspectors a lot of extra work. Other measures implemented after KPMG's report are training staff in shaking hands correctly and sending questions to the animal owner immediately

after the inspection to ask how they experienced the inspection. The Food Safety Authority receives approximately 12,000 tips about poor animal welfare annually. The Food Safety Authority has recently established labor-intensive routines for assessing the received concern reports. A lot of resources are used to categorize and sort these tips, but there are few resources to follow up, even serious shortcomings, with inspections. The Food Safety Authority's excessive internal control also contributes to great frustration.

The example shows how the quality of services was reduced following the new NPM-inspired routines. The layering of control routines creates new administrative tasks perceived as meaningless by the workers. Accountability for delivered results is given disproportionate weight compared to ensuring good service delivery and, such as in the above case, ensuring actual animal welfare, one of the agency's core tasks. Reports about service delivery are adjusted mainly to look good, but performing such empty rituals only for control purposes and not to support the employees in their work is demotivating for workers.

This is not a unique example. Excessive control affects all sectors. The final report from the SAMRISK project, which examined how NPM works for critical infrastructure, and thus for societal security in organizations responsible for electricity networks, water supply, information, and communication technology, concluded that NPM-inspired organizational changes led to greater formalization of work and fragmentation of organizations. It harmed the informal networks between different professionals, which are important for improvisation in critical situations. Again, the formalization, fragmentation, and increased red tape took attention away from operational work (Almklov et al., 2011). Kuldova (2022) describes the proliferation of such compliance-oriented pseudo-solutions in response to both the regulatory state, NPM, and digital revolution, which, together, perpetually generate the need for more control and more compliance, while paying little attention to what kind of a society these management and control systems are creating. They may make the world measurable, comparable, evaluation-friendly, but they do not necessarily make it more controllable. Likelier, they just make it flat and meaningless, without diversity and variation. The control systems also do not solve the promised societal challenges they were supposed to alleviate. At the same time, scandals are used to push through the introduction of increasingly intrusive regulation supported by technology. Anything informal is considered a risk that must be brought under control (Kuldova, 2022).

Public health organizations also suffer from this enthusiasm for production and control. Standardized care pathways may look promising from a macro perspective, but may create problems at the individual level because standardized treatment cannot be adapted to the individual as easily. Despite their failures, these control systems are seductive, as they appear sensible and simple. The theory provides a comprehensible explanation of how results can be achieved and seemingly offers the ability to maintain control. At the same time, this need for control creates problems in practice. The more top-down control there is, the more rigid and less adapted to reality the systems become. In the long run, these control systems create unsustainable workplaces and reduce the quality of services provided—a system where neither patients nor workers thrive.

Falkum (2020) has documented in detail how the state has strengthened control in work organizations. While authoritarian and top-down control regimes are not new, paradoxically, with liberalism, some of this control returned and we have witnessed a growth of top-down control and resurgence of authoritarian modes of management. MBOR was originally intended to replace rule management in the public sector (Drucker [1954] 2012), but what is today referred to as MBOR shares similarities with the bureaucratic rule management that Drucker's ideas were supposed to be an alternative to. Goal management has become integrated as a new layer of rule management.

The Co-determination Survey from the Work Research Institute showed that control in the public—also to a large degree private—sector is increasingly detail-oriented with many and clear goals and objectives. Everyone has been measured on these detail-oriented goals (Falkum et al., 2022). The goals are so detail-oriented that they fail to capture the sectors or the companies' overall objectives and mission. Both managers and employees try to live up to indicators they are measured by, but which often deviate strongly from the actual main objectives of the organization. This, in turn, contributes to public organizations failing to fulfill their societal missions.

Neoliberal control systems rely on the fundamental belief that organization based on the principles of performance, competition, and individual interests increases productivity. This type of organization stands in contrast to social democratic thinking, which puts solidarity, cooperation, and collective interests at the forefront. Control, which does not take into account the real nature and needs of humans, only rarely produces good results, and can lead to bad ones, dissatisfaction, and stress among employees. Increased control and surveillance in workplaces affect employees' opportunities to influence their own work situation. The conditions for co-determination have gradually worsened over time. The Work Research Institutes' *Co-determination Survey* for 2022 showed that public companies' use of consulting firms, instead of deliberating with union representatives, serves as an integral part of this control. The practice leads to a depoliticization and abdication of responsibility. Management depends on hired experts and consultants instead of deliberating with employee representatives. Using consulting firms can be a way of shying away from accountability. The management can, with consultant reports backing them, argue that they have a knowledge-based decision-making basis, and this makes decisions appear neutral. Political decisions can, in this way, be turned into questions of expert knowledge and thus be depoliticized.

Digitalization further strengthens this control. Digital and technological tools primarily support management and administration's need for control. They are seldom primarily constructed to help and support employees in their work. Instead, they tend to be geared towards control, monitoring, and surveillance. This further strengthens the ethos and institutional logic of the management and administration. In theory, regulations should remain unaffected by digitalization, but technology is not neutral nor objective. Regulations are in practice adapted to be digitalization-friendly. In practice, this means that digitalization shapes regulations rather than the other way round (Falkum et al., 2022).

The development in the public sector has shifted from an emphasis on the leadership of organizations to an increased emphasis on control (Byrkjeflot, 1997), and has gone hand-in-hand with the aforementioned market orientation in the public sector and regulation through MBOR. This regulation narrows the possibilities for real co-determination, or collective power to challenge control systems (Falkum et al., 2022). When digitization is layered on top of these systems, it enhances the control and monitoring of what and how it is done. This control has negative side effects. Detailed requirements and control of what has been done reduces professionals' autonomy in how to solve tasks and undermines professional discretion. This contributes to feelings of powerlessness and dissatisfaction among employees (Hari, 2020).

Formally, the number of working hours required has not changed and is still regulated by the provisions of the Working Environment Act.[2] But the content of work has changed, which, in turn, increases the pressure on working hours. Employees are faced with new requirements and quantitative and qualitative goals, new regulatory requirements, and incentive schemes, such as quality assurance, evaluation, reporting, risk assessment, and implementation of new technological solutions, security and privacy routines, new applications, and templates. Employees must deal with and fulfill all of this. Working hour regulations come under subtle pressure from the increasing amount of rules and digital processes that must be adhered to. Employers do not ask employees to work more. Rather, employees work more hours because their normal workday is not long enough to stick to all these control procedures. It is the market orientation of the public sector over several years that has created this situation.

Higher education and research are organized to ensure publication in international scientific journals, and teaching is designed for greater throughput of pupils and students, the so-called "credit points production" (Tjora, 2019; Kuldova, 2021). The Quality Reform in Higher Education has also resulted in more commissions and more tightly governed research. What to research is determined by those who provide the funding, while allocations for basic research are decreasing. The outcome of the research (impact) must be described in detail by the researchers in order to receive funding. In this way, those who finance the research control the outcome. The funders follow up closely, through contracts, that what is ordered gets produced and that certain procedures, related to methods, ethics, and privacy, are adhered to throughout the research process. Such formalization around consent can seem intimidating to researchers' informants and prevent them from speaking freely. The argument for this type of organization is to ensure that money is spent on useful research and that privacy is sufficiently maintained. However, what is useful is debatable. It is not certain that policymakers and administrative employees should always define what research to conduct. Ultimately, in the long run, this organization could threaten the production of independent and free research, including system-critical research.

The very foundation of research and innovation is built on trial, error, contemplation, and reflection. There is less time for this now. The research process itself is more tightly controlled. Researchers must use predefined

[2] https://lovdata.no/dokument/NLE/lov/2005-06-17-62

templates and descriptions of how the research should be conducted and apply for permissions for what they can do and how (Hall & Winlow, 2012). Teaching has also changed, as the focus is on throughput. Students no longer attend lectures that are rumored to be interesting. They rush through the student factory to collect as many points as quickly as possible. Both students and the university are rewarded for this. Independent thinking is increasingly drowning in production figures of graduated students, points for research production, and the number of doctorates. There is little room for trial, error, and innovation in such a system. Thus, researchers also remain inside the box. The scarcity of innovative thinking is a problem in a time when we need to think system-critically in order to move towards a more socially and environmentally sustainable society (Giroux, 2007, 2009, 2020; Berg et al., 2016; Loveday, 2018). More resources are spent on applying for funding and proposals than what is finally allocated to research. An evaluation of research institutes in Norway has shown that the OECD believes it to be a challenge for long-term knowledge building that direct public funding is under 20% of Norwegian research institutes' revenues (The Research Council of Norway, 2018).

Centralized Public Procurement, Competition, and Management Through Contracts

In the public sector, tenders are often about winning framework agreements—i.e., an exclusive right to deliver specific goods or services throughout the period of the agreement (normally up to four years). The competitions are often large and many public organizations collaborate in the tenders, which come with a number of requirements. For example, it may be required that the supplier must deliver nationwide, in large quantities, and year-round.

Collaboration on large contracts means that public organizations can press on prices. These large tenders and contracts can also instill a feeling of safety because it is easier to avoid criticism for favoring specific suppliers at the local level. Larger contracts can also be practical in terms of time management and logistics, but this management and control can create sustainability challenges. Non-profit organizations and small- and medium-sized companies struggle to compete in these large tenders for public contracts. Even though non-profit organizations can provide both qualitative and economic benefits to society that go beyond the benefits they provide in the delivery of the specific service the competition is announced for, they are not winning these large contracts. The social sustainability that non-profit organizations provide is seldom valued in these competitions and falls outside the contracts' scope. These types of values are difficult to emphasize in the way procurement is practiced today.[3]

Public tenders and contracts can become so large that they, in practice, exclude smaller businesses from participation. The Norwegian Division for Public Procurement[4] is growing, signing exclusive framework contracts on behalf of 190 state organizations, and now also for municipalities and county municipalities. The size of the contracts is also increasing. The Norwegian Division for Public Procurement enters into and manages joint framework contracts for state enterprises. These are mandatory for all state administrative bodies in the civil sector. It is very hard for a subordinate organization, such as a university, to opt out and buy from someone else. The Norwegian Division for Public Procurement sends the tender documents out for consultation, but opting out from such agreements is up to the centralized procurement department of the organization (like a university). Any subordinate department or organization must comply. The large exclusive framework contracts—i.e., with travel agencies and catering companies—limit leaders' and other employees' possibility to buy products and services that they need for their work. The contracts are meant to make the procedures simpler and cheaper, but are often experienced as a burden, increasing the cost for each employee. There is little practical opportunity to opt out and choose another supplier or to give feedback on the product and services delivered. The way is long to the central procurement department.

Centralized public tenders give few opportunities to bid on parts of a competition. The practical consequence is that larger suppliers are favored, and smaller suppliers get pushed out of the market.[5] The procurement practice, where small actors are excluded, is maintained through requirements that are more difficult to reach for small suppliers with less administrative capacity than for bigger companies. It is too much administrative work for them to participate in the competition, and they often prefer to

---

[3] "Smartere innkjøp – effektive og profesjonelle offentlige anskaffelser," Meld. St. 22 (2018–2019). https://www.regjeringen.no/contentassets/2d7006f67c374cbdab5d4d6ba7198ebd/no/pdfs/stm201820190022000dddpdfs.pdf

[4] https://anskaffelser.no/velkommen-til-statens-innkjopssenter

[5] "Smartere innkjøp – effektive og profesjonelle offentlige anskaffelser," Meld. St. 22 (2018–2019). https://www.regjeringen.no/contentassets/2d7006f67c374cbdab5d4d6ba7198ebd/no/pdfs/stm201820190022000dddpdfs.pdf

sell their products to large wholesalers. The competition is also unfair in the marketplace. To take the example of food, the prices that large food actors buy for are often lower than those of the independent smaller actors, as the former can pressure suppliers on price. Centralized procurement can be practical, but often leads to a standardized selection of goods and services that does not suit anyone's specific needs. This is a problem for hotels, florists, and a range of other goods and services.[6] For example, staying at an independent hotel in Bergen that employs people in work training and that only serves local food is not allowed if the public organization you work for has a framework agreement with the largest hotel chain in the Nordic region. Instead of buying locally produced food, many municipalities end up buying food transported from far away because they have restraints on who they buy from in these framework agreements. This happens even if the municipality itself is a large meat or vegetable producing location. Public organizations are not always good at checking that they get the quality they pay for, and how well suppliers deliver is seldom a criterion in future tenders. In practice, one of the most important reasons for framework agreements is not necessarily price, but to control how employees purchase and prevent them from spending work time on procurement.

However, there is leeway in the law for procurement to enter into open contracts that are not exclusive. Public organizations can divide contracts and give the opportunity to subordinate organizations, such as schools and nursing homes, to be their own procurement unit. Juggling the regulations and doing this correctly, however, requires a competence and understanding of regulations and resources that procurement departments in smaller municipalities often do not have. It is also difficult for procurement units to see how procurement should be rigged so that they do not end up in situations where they exceed threshold values—maximum sums allowed to buy from the same supplier. Centralized procurement departments add the sum of all procurement from all schools, kindergartens, nursing homes, and organizations in the municipality to calculate threshold values. This brings the total sum up and often requires tendering contracts at the EU level, which is extensive and administratively demanding. Nevertheless, decentralizing purchases makes it harder to reach threshold

---

[6] "Smartere innkjøp – effektive og profesjonelle offentlige anskaffelser," Meld. St. 22 (2018–2019). https://www.regjeringen.no/contentassets/2d7006f67c374cbdab5d4d6ba7198ebd/no/pdfs/stm201820190022000dddpdfs.pdf

values, but also reduces central control over procurement and deviates from the efficiency and digitization strategy of the procurement policy. Therefore, giving more freedom to subordinate units so that, for example, nursing homes can buy local Norwegian apples during the season becomes more complicated than expected (Muromskaya, 2022).

Outsourcing tasks and organizing for competition is meant to bring about the best candidates to do the job in the most efficient and economical way. However, the question is whether outsourcing always produces the best solutions in all industries at all times, or if this system hinders better and more innovative solutions. The question is also whether the system itself becomes disproportionately expensive to operate. When tenders favor bigger companies, this can also lead to the monopolization of the marketplace and the creation of oligopolies. Christina Meyer and Victor Norman, affiliated with the Conservative Party, confronted this competition logic and last decade's reforms in the public sector in their book, arguing that the public sector has a different social role than the private (Meyer & Norman, 2019), and therefore should not be organized like a private company.

References

Almklov, P. G., Antonsen, S., & Fenstad, J. (2011). *NPM, Kritiske infrastrukturer og samfunnssikkerhet*. https://www.sintef.no/globalassets/project/nexus/npm-kritisk-infrastruktur-2-utgave-trykkeriet-180211.pdf

Amundsen, C. S. (2022). Markedsstyringens konsekvenser i den offentlige velferdssektoren. *Nordic Journal of Wellbeing and Sustainable Welfare Development, 1*(1), 67–71. https://doi.org/10.18261/njwel.1.1.6

Berg, L. D., Huijbens, E. H., & Larsen, H. G. (2016). Producing Anxiety in the Neoliberal University. *The Canadian Geographer, 60*(2), 168–180. https://doi.org/10.1111/cag.12261

Byrkjeflot, H. (Ed.). (1997). *Fra styring til ledelse*. Fagbokforlaget.

Claro, S., Paunesku, D., & Dweck, C. S. (2016). Growth Mindset Tempers the Effects of Poverty on Academic Achievement. *Proceedings of the National Academy of Sciences, 113*(31), 8664–8668. https://doi.org/10.1073/pnas.1608207113

Drucker, P. (2012). *The Practice of Management*. Routledge.

Falkum, E. (2020). *Makt og opposisjon i arbeidslivet: Maktforskyvninger fra 1900 til 2020*. Cappelen Damm Akademisk.

Falkum, E., Nordrik, B., Wathne, C. T., Drange, I., Hansen, P. B., Dahl, E. M., Kuldova, T., & Underthun, A. (2022). *Måling og styring av arbeidstid–Medbestemmelsesbarometeret 2021*. AFI-rapport 2022, 01.

Giroux, H. A. (2007). Beyond Neoliberal Common Sense: Cultural Politics and Public Pedagogy in Dark Times. *JAC, 27*(1/2), 11–61.
Giroux, H. A. (2009). Democracy's Nemesis: The Rise of the Corporate University. *Cultural Studies—Critical Methodologies, 9*(5), 669–695. https://doi.org/10.1177/1532708609341169
Giroux, H. A. (2020). *Neoliberalism's War on Higher Education*. Haymarket Books.
Hall, S., & Winlow, S. (2012). What is an 'Ethics Committee'? *The British Journal of Criminology, 52*(2), 400–416. https://doi.org/10.1093/bjc/azr082
Hari, J. (2020). *Lost Connections*. Bloomsbury Publishing.
Hood, C., & Dixon, R. (2015). *A Government that Worked Better and Cost Less? Evaluating Three Decades of Reform and Change in UK Central Government*. Oxford University Press. https://doi.org/10.1093/acprof:oso/9780199687022.001.0001
Innset, O. (2020). *Markedsvendingen: Nyliberalismens historie i Norge*. Fagbokforlaget.
Kuldova, T. Ø. (2021). The Cynical University: Gamified Subjectivity in Norwegian Academia. *Ephemera: Theory & Politics in Organization, 21*(3), 1–29.
Kuldova, T. Ø. (2022). *Compliance-Industrial Complex: The Operating System of a Pre-Crime Society*. Palgrave Pivot. https://doi.org/10.1007/978-3-031-19224-1
Loveday, V. (2018). The Neurotic Academic: Anxiety, Casualisation, and Governance in the Neoliberalising University. *Journal of Cultural Economy, 11*(2), 154–166. https://doi.org/10.1080/17530350.2018.1426032
Madsen, O. J. (2020). *Livsmestring på timeplanen—Rett medisin for elevene?* Spartacus.
Meyer, C., & Norman, V. (2019). *Ikke for å konkurrere. Strategi for fellesskapets tjenere*. Fagbokforlaget.
Muromskaya, M. (2022). Hvorfor klarer ikke kommunene å kjøpe inn lokal og bærekraftig mat? *Forskning.no*, 17. October 2022.
Nordkvelle, Y., & Nyhus, L. (2017). Management by Objectives as an Administrative Strategy in Norwegian Schools: Interpretations and Judgements in Contrived Liberation. In N. Veggeland (Ed.), *Administrative Strategies of our Time* (pp. 219–260). Nova Science Publishers.
Reegård, K., & Rogstad, J. (Eds.). (2016). *De frafalne: Om frafall i videregående opplæring—Hvem er de, hva vil de og hva kan gjøres?* Gyldendal.
Ryan, R. M., & Deci, E. L. (2000). Intrinsic and Extrinsic Motivations: Classic Definitions and New Directions. *Contemporary Educational Psychology, 25*(1), 54–67. https://doi.org/10.1006/ceps.1999.1020
The Research Council of Norway. (2018). *En målrettet og effektiv instituttpolitikk. En systematisk gjennomgang av forskningsrådets evaluering av forskningsinstitutter*. Synteserapport.
Tjora, A. (2019). (red.) *Universitetskamp*. Scandinavian Academic Press.

CHAPTER 5

New Public Management in Urban Governance

Abstract Urban development in Norway is regulated through law, but is carried out locally by municipalities. Oslo, the capital of Norway, is growing and constantly needs more housing to meet demand. Therefore, a densification policy is pursued. In Norway, private developers and property owners have the most influence over urban development. Big decisions in urban development are established in contracts between the municipality and property developers before residents are invited to state their opinion. The responsibility for participation has been delegated to developers. The lack of arenas for early participation from the local community is one of the biggest democratic challenges in today's urban development. Participation could have been a tool to contribute to more socially sustainable cities, but only 20% of residents report that municipal participation channels actually give them influence.

Keywords Urban Development · Participation · The Commons · Gentrification · Planning · Local Community

What opportunities do you have, as a resident, to influence local community development? We can take an illustrative example from Skøyen, an area in Oslo. It is built densely and perhaps in a way that does not primarily focus on the well-being of residents and visitors. When you drive on

© The Author(s), under exclusive license to Springer Nature Switzerland AG 2025
K. Reichborn-Kjennerud, *Sustainable Urban Transitions and New Public Management,*
https://doi.org/10.1007/978-3-031-82307-7_5

Hoffsveien towards Skøyen, the protected charming old house Sofienlund, a former country house, looks small and cramped in front of the enormous office buildings towering in the background. The tallest office building steals solar heat from many homes behind it, and is a building that needs cooling systems due to the lack of shading elements. The property value was so high after the petrol station that stood on the plot was demolished that the developer had to add many floors to profit from the project, according to discussions among residents who debated the issue on the Facebook group Urban Developers.[1] The many tall buildings pressed together in a tiny area visually overwhelm the small listed building. This is the result of the densification policy that was supposed to be environmentally and socially sustainable, but which perhaps ended up being only economically sustainable for a few select actors (Sørgjerd, 2018).

Another example is Bjørvika. Politicians had visions of a socially and environmentally sustainable project with affordable housing, but the result differed from their political vision. Bjørvika bears more the mark of having been designed for accounting and law firms, and wealthy visitors than socially diverse and open to all. Often, the municipality takes little responsibility for planning, design, and development and we end up with solutions defined by market actors that do not reflect the vision politicians set in the first place (Andersen & Røe, 2017). At the same time, the outdoor areas in Sørenga, in front of the Oslo Opera House and behind the Munch Museum, open up the seafront areas to the population. In this case, politicians succeeded in prioritizing the commons. The new Oslo Public Library (Deichman) in Bjørvika has won an international award for the best public library in 2021, and has become the grand living room for all of Oslo.

We encountered the same conflict between business- and resident-friendly urban development in the aforementioned Democratic urban development in the digital age (DEMUDIG) research project. As expressed by a resident:

> I live in an area where traffic and business interests historically weigh heavier than the interests of the population. We have active local groups and wonderful enthusiasts who have been engaged for several decades (from 1970) without ever being heard.

---

[1] https://www.dagsavisen.no/debatt/2019/01/14/utbygging-av-skoyen-ta-vare-pa-sjoen-og-strandomradene/

Major decisions are often already made and enshrined in contracts between the municipality and property developers before the two invite residents to participate. Contractual agreements can ensure efficient and rapid housing construction that the city needs, but often comes at the expense of quality and good solutions. As another resident expressed:

> I think many politicians are too concerned with profit and capital. They do not see what gentrification and very dense construction do to residential areas.

Contracts that have already been entered into are hard to change without excessively high costs for the municipality. Thus, participation becomes difficult and is often perceived as pretend or make-believe democracy because it requires a disproportionate amount of time, competence, and a large network of influential people to make an impact in important matters. The fact that it has become possible to participate digitally has not opened the democratic space to more groups. Instead, competent super-users must also use this channel to try to promote residents' interests in urban development (Legard et al., 2021). Most people experience participation as a legitimization of decisions that have already been made. Power is unevenly distributed, and 75% of politicians and 65% of employees working with urban development and participation in Oslo municipality believe that developers and property owners have the most influence in urban development (Legard et al., 2021; Dokk Holm, 2021). Participation is also challenging because it is difficult to find good representatives for all interests in an area.

Although this example may demonstrate how profits can come at the expense of sustainability, market organization has historically also come with some good and democratizing effects. The *bourgeoisie* overthrew the hegemony of the nobility through its newfound wealth. Thus, markets and capitalist systems contributed to reducing earlier privileges. The nobility had property, but the bourgeoisie owned the means of production and opportunities were created for new population groups through the power of money (perhaps to a lesser extent in Norway, which had little to no nobility). At the same time, capitalism has a destabilizing effect on society because capital tends to accumulate and benefit a small percentage of the population (Piketty, 2014). After the industrialization in the twentieth century, the role of the state has therefore historically been to balance capitalism using various methods. However, it becomes a danger to democracy if the state itself begins behaving like a capitalist. Market logic as a governing principle in the state can lead to values such as profit being emphasized more than democracy and equality before the law (Innset, 2020; Voldnes, 2012a, 2012b).

However, the introduction of market mechanisms in the state since the 1980s is partly due to challenges with the previous system that did not meet voters' expectations. In the 1970s, there were constant budget overruns, and the public sector was perceived as rigid, bureaucratic, and unresponsive to citizens. Professions largely controlled how resources were used in public agencies, and New Public Management (NPM) was designed to break this power of the professions. Less centralization and bureaucracy were to make the state more oriented towards the users. This is one of the reasons why Management by Objectives and Results (MBOR) was introduced as a management principle in Norway as of the 1990s. Focusing on overarching goals, the system was to create more room for action locally in public organizations and reduce micro-management. NPM was initially introduced to curb bureaucracy and centralization. The desire was for a more responsive and user-oriented public sector, but the result turned out to be the opposite in some cases.

As discussed earlier in this book, the reforms have, in some areas, worked as intended, but have had a number of unintended negative side effects (Busch et al., 2004). Much suggests that NPM led to more centralization and unnecessary work by controlling, measuring, and weighing everything state employees do (Grund, 2019). Some reforms have been implemented precisely as detailed activity management so that room for action, which had been promised, disappeared. In many cases, NPM tools ended up being an empty ritual where employees work to satisfy the system rather than the users (Grund, 2019). According to new research, there has been a tendency, over time, for public organizations to manage and control their employees harder. The professions in various jobs have also lost much of their power to administrative systems that focus primarily on profits and cost control (Linder et al., 2018). Digitization, employee surveillance, and the use of regulatory technology reinforce this tendency (Kuldova, 2022; Falkum et al., 2022). Through various reporting and standardization regimes, risk assessments, best practice guides, and ethical guidelines implemented in digital systems, the detailed control and surveillance of employees and users are enabled. This increased control has created a market for companies that can deliver digital solutions for security and surveillance (Dwyer, 2022). Companies with expertise in regulation and technology then provide input to legislation that again creates a need for more control systems (Kuldova, 2022). Management in public organizations is increasingly about compliance with formal standards and rules and less room is given to actual professional discretion and management (Kuldova, 2022). Even the concept of sustainability is co-opted by regulatory technology, made into indicators and subject to machine compliance and control. Sustainability thus creates a new market for companies in regulatory technology and compliance.

This development towards ever more management and control can be understood through the term "governmentality" (Foucault, 1975). The modern state is constructed as a panopticon, a surveillance tower in the middle of a prison, where the guards can see all the cells standing in a circle around the tower, but the prisoners do not see the observer so they cannot know when they are being watched. Because the prisoners know that they are being watched, they begin to self-correct to avoid being punished by the prison guards. Governmentality, in its essence, thus becomes a governance of the mind, or "governance of the soul" (Rose, 1999), and is a governance tool in modern states. Bureaucratic systems monitor and control the population so that they stay comfortable enough not to revolt and obedient enough to contribute in a way that maintains the status quo. The question is whether this control can become too strong so that it feels increasingly uncomfortable. This control can become so inhibiting for human development and well-being that it can lead to health issues or other negative behavioral effects. Even though it is possible to control a population effectively with modern tools, humans are more than machines. Humans need community, a creative outlet, and to use their abilities. This is where social sustainability is relevant, since social and environmental sustainability contribute in many subtle ways to increased well-being and thus, to better public health. Increasing control and detailed monitoring can have the opposite effect, namely the feeling of being isolated in competition with others. This in turn can cause stress reactions and a feeling of time scarcity (Hari, 2020).

Democracy in Urban Development

Urban development affects people's living conditions in many ways, including their health, welfare, and social life. The UN concept of social sustainability encompasses these values and points to considerations that must be taken for residential environments, social life, and area development. Additionally, the concept of sustainability emphasizes features of local communities relevant for democracy, such as social capital, participation, and networks, reciprocity, and trust between neighbors. Good urban development can have positive effects on many such life areas that fall under the UN's sustainability concept.

The framework for urban development is set by law and guidelines at the national level, but city and local community development are carried out locally by municipalities. Even though residents have some opportunities to influence decisions directly through hearings and other initiatives where they are invited to express their opinions, questions can be raised about how effective or democratic these tools for participatory democracy actually are and who, in practice, gets the opportunity to provide input.

Urban development that actually includes residents' perspectives—as well as policy—is just as important as participation. Participatory democracy cannot solve principled political questions—i.e., what kind of society and city do we want to live in, and create for future generations? Participation is therefore not sufficient. Sustainability measures are also not always best taken care of through local participation. Restrictions on car use and facilitation for the commons may be less popular among some residents. At the same time, organizations that advocate for the local community's interests can contribute to more resident-friendly solutions, such as local parks being prioritized over denser and higher residential and commercial buildings, which in isolation, favor developers' profitability, but also lessen social sustainability.

Prioritizing aesthetics in the built environment is also important for sustainability, but does not abide to market logic. Our built environments affect well-being. This is what the *Arkitekturopprøret* (Architecture Rebellion), an initiative by residents who feel alienated by the shiny, tall facades and dead outdoor spaces, warns about.[2] Building ugly is not sustainable. If human considerations are not taken into account and buildings are built too densely, the buildings will have to be demolished sooner than necessary. An example of this is the urban renewal in Grünerløkka, a central district of Oslo, in the 1980s, where residential blocks in the inner courtyards were demolished. Considerations for good outdoor spaces and meeting places, light, spaciousness, living space, and kitchens are under pressure from market forces to this day.

[2] https://www.arkitekturopproret.no/

Densification Policy

NPM reforms impact society in similar ways across different sectors. More power is given to the private market in all sectors, and this is also the case in urban development. One reason why the municipality of Oslo has transferred more power to private developers is the fact that the city is growing and is in constant need of more housing to meet demand. Therefore, a densification policy is pursued to gather people around transport hubs, and preserve the local forest and arable land. In addition, former industrial areas, like in Nydalen and Kværnerbyen, are being converted into residential areas. However, transferring power to developers makes it harder to plan holistically.

Urban development in Norway is highly deregulated. Developers have been given responsibility for most of the detailed planning in the initial developing phases and in the execution of construction processes. Thus, the need for profit is shaping the urban space, leading to less resident-friendly solutions (Andersen & Røe, 2017; Legard et al., 2021). Developers have no interest in preserving the commons, so holistic area development becomes harder to achieve, as it is more profitable for businesses to build as densely as possible. The importance of the commons, such as parks close to residential areas, then becomes more difficult to prioritize. Residents are usually allowed to give input in the final phase of the projects when the most important decisions have already been made. There are few examples of residents providing input at the start of projects (Hanssen, 2013; Sæter & Ruud, 2005; Dahlgren et al., 2021).

Social Sustainability from Residents' Perspective

It is difficult for residents to influence urban development, as demonstrated by a quote from the DEMUDIG research project. Here, a resident shares how she experiences participation in urban development in a downtown district in Melbourne:

> I only ever see the knocking down of beautiful things, even if it's just a nice spacious dirt car park, and replacing it with something awful, hideous, massive, less convenient, in the name of either profit (replacing houses with apartment buildings where the apartments have no personality and maximize the number of rooms per apartment) or personal gain via saying they made something environmentally friendly like a horrible asphalt car park

built out of recycled crap. No one consults anyone, asking if these things are what the community wants. People in councils or in the administration just have ideas and want to do it their way because they resent the residents.

Is urban development experienced as the quote above illustrates? If so, there is reason to ask how well democracy, and thus social sustainability, is maintained in urban development. Democracy is understood here as a fair system for negotiating between different interests in an area, where the majority makes decisions, while taking into account the rights of the minority. By fair is meant that the correct process is followed and that the result is good for the parties involved.

In the DEMUDIG project, we examined how well participatory democracy works in urban and local community development and asked questions, such as who has the power in urban development policy and how can residents possibly gain more influence? (Hovik et al., 2022a, 2022b; Legard et al., 2021, 2022). We studied central urban areas because the population there is more diverse than in more homogeneous residential areas on the city outskirts. In the central districts, there is also more competition for space because businesses and property developers have interests in these areas. In the project, politicians, municipal employees, and residents shared their perceptions of participation and influence in urban development. The five central districts in Oslo were compared with central districts in Madrid and Melbourne. In both cities, residents have lower trust in their politicians than in Norway, while local authorities have opened up for more participation than in Oslo, especially through digital platforms (Hovik et al., 2022a).

The Power of the Systems

In the organization of urban development lies significant power with implications for the final result. The question thus becomes how laws and democratic decisions are actually operationalized through the systems we have today. In Norway, urban development is more neoliberal and developer-driven than in the other Nordic countries (Nordahl et al., 2008).

Norway's governance system is enshrined in the state's financial regulations. Governance specific to urban development is implemented through the *Planning and Building Act*, the *Municipal Act*, and detailed more through municipal, overarching, and zoning plans. The latter are the responsibility of municipal politicians as they are adopted by municipal councils. However, it is private developers that propose the zoning plans in about 90% of cases in Norway, which gives them significant influence on how the actual solutions end up looking. This falls in line with the emergence of the Norwegian "regulatory state" (Veggeland, 2009, 2010) that others have analyzed in a global context (Kuldova, 2022).

The municipal plan is overarching, while the zoning plans are more concrete. It is at the zoning plan stage that it becomes clear to residents what will actually happen in their area, but at this step in the process, the minimum requirement for participation is the announcement of initiation and hearing. However, the hearing phase comes too late in the process for residents to have the opportunity to significantly influence the result (Hanssen, 2013).

One of our resident respondents expressed the lack of opportunity to influence like this:

> The formal channels are too fragmented and inaccessible. I have been part of the management of a hearing body for [three] years and still do not understand what is what. It is set up so that less resourceful people are not able make their voices heard.

The quote illustrates how difficult it is, even for people who have experience with the system, to understand what can be done to gain influence through the hearing institute. It is then not surprising that the silent voices who do not have resources and competence on the way the system works struggle to have their voices heard in urban development. The question is also whether hearing responses from individuals is given equal weight, compared, for instance, to professionally executed hearing responses from interest organizations, lobbying from companies, and so on.

Developers have little interest in the holistic planning and in the neighborhood-oriented thinking that physical planning posits as an ideal (Fimreite & Medalen, 2005). At the same time, the greatest responsibility for involving residents is placed on developers, who submit the planning proposals and have been delegated the responsibility for participation in the new *Planning and Building Act* of 2008 in Norway. However, those who take this responsibility normally only meet the minimum requirements of the law. Therefore, the authorities have less power and opportunity to ensure that participation and the commons are maintained than if these tasks had remained a public responsibility. Public planning authorities also have limited resources to follow-up on how participation is actually safeguarded and solved by the developers, and have no possibilities for sanctions. The lack of arenas to involve residents from local communities early in the planning phase is one of the biggest democratic challenges in today's urban development in Norway (Hanssen, 2013).

At the same time, the law's intention is that participation should be the basis for all planning and urban development (Hanssen, 2013). In other words, the letter of the law is followed, but not its spirit. This lack of organization for inhabitants' influence is similar to the development of corporate democracy in public organizations, which have also become more market-oriented. Productivity takes precedence over democracy, and co-determination is in practice replaced by participation, which significantly weakens corporate democracy (Falkum et al., 2022). Union representatives' role is reduced to participation that merely legitimizes choices the management makes, sometimes referred to as pseudo-democracy by critical union representatives (Kuldova et al., 2020). At the same time, developers, unlike state employers, are market actors with special interests. They do not prioritize democracy, and cannot be expected to take responsibility for it.

Entrepreneurial Cities

Municipalities exist in a global market, and they have become entrepreneurial to attract resources. They build opera and cultural houses to attract investments, innovative workers, and resourceful residents, labelled "the creative class" by Richard Florida (2012). Rising housing prices and general inflation can be the consequences of such development, driving the gentrification processes that push residents and smaller businesses out to the periphery. This development is global (Lees et al., 2016), where local authorities drive an active investment policy to attract the right population groups to urban centres. Market considerations become important in the planning and management of cities, often at the expense of residents' interests (Lees et al., 2016).

Participation could have been used as a tool to contribute to more socially sustainable cities, but the fact that developers have been given the main responsibility for participation is a key obstacle to such noble visions. Not only are they less concerned with participation than local politicians, but have also no business interest in participation. Only 23% of municipal employees responsible for planning feel that developers take responsibility for ensuring participation at an early stage. At the same time, the municipality should ensure that developers take responsibility for participation in zoning plans (Hanssen, 2013). The question, however, is how effective are the tools they have for safeguarding participation, and how many resources do they have to ensure this actually gets done? For example, municipal employees have no sanctions they can use against developers who do not take responsibility for participation.

As a consequence, many residents spend a lot of time trying to steer urban development in a resident-friendly direction, but are invited to express their opinions so late in the process that they are seen as reactive and protesting. If participation had been organized more in advance of the process, they could have contributed valuable local knowledge with input on what ensures good living and urban quality, possibly contributing to more creative and proactive solutions (Hanssen, 2013). However, the question is whether there is a real interest in this type of input that could make urban areas qualitatively better to live in.

Residents and politicians are obliged to comply with the already signed and agreed upon development contracts and planning proposals. They find it difficult to say "no" to a planning proposal that the parties have spent several years formulating. Therefore, representative democracy also does not safeguard residents' interests. Moreover, 37% of local politicians feel committed to planning proposals, while only 7% feel bound by hearing statements, and 13% by public meetings (Hanssen, 2013). Research has thus documented that representative democracy and participation, through the hearing institute, are not sufficient to ensure real participation and influence in the governance system that the state and municipalities operate within today. Developers' plans take precedence over residents' interests, and over those of citizens and society as whole.

Opportunity to Secure the Commons and Physical Meeting Places

Examples of commons and public spaces in cities where people can meet and are free of charge include parks, libraries, and other public indoor or outdoor spaces. Such public spaces should have certain characteristics, such as diversity and the absence of hierarchy. They are for all groups and types of people, and contribute to well-being and democratic expression (Sennett, 2005; Amin, 2008). It is the public sector's responsibility, on behalf of the population, to maintain and manage such commons. Public spaces are places that can train people in tolerance for diversity and in citizenship. They are common goods for citizens, where your role is not just to be an individual and a consumer with private interests. They are arenas for social learning (Amin & Thrift, 2002). However, the goal of the current NPM-inspired organization of the public sector is not to maintain the commons, but to increase cost efficiency, and produce faster and better public goods and services. Therefore, the question is whether the commons and democracy are maintained well enough within such a system, where this type of consideration may be hard to prioritize (Hermansen, 2013).

Commons, which are free and open to all, have been under pressure for a while. Don Mitchell described in *The Right to The City* how security measures in New York have made more areas and parks inaccessible (Mitchell, 2003). In Norway, we also have large areas owned and operated privately, such as the company Avantor in Nydalen.[3] The privatization of areas opens the possibility for excluding certain groups. Mitchell gives several examples of how this happens, with security as justification, arguing that public places must remain public and explaining that equal access to public spaces in cities ensures social justice (Mitchell, 2003).

Certain security measures can nevertheless contribute to public spaces becoming available to more people. One can argue that a place is not really publicly available to everyone if it is taken over, for example, by drug dealers. At the same time, security measures can have negative consequences if people are always seen as a potential threat rather than as fellow citizens. Hostile architecture, or disciplinary architecture, discourages social engagement and makes prolonged stays in public spaces difficult. Such security-driven measures are partly based on assumptions about crime, and criminologists have pointed out that this trend reflects the individualization of society (Raymen, 2015). However, the right to the city also depends on it being there for more than just the economically affluent to live in (Reichborn-Kjennerud, 2016). Workers, nurses, teachers, and other wage earners should also be able to live in the city with the wages they earn, so that they do not have to spend large parts of the day commuting back and forth. The city becoming too expensive for workers is part of the phenomenon of gentrification. Increased property values in former working-class areas price out tenants with medium to low wages, so they are eventually forced to move out. This happens all over the globe (Lees et al., 2016), and is hardly socially sustainable to promote

---

[3] https://www.dagsavisen.no/nyheter/innenriks/2004/11/21/nydalen-en-privat-bydel-med-diktatorisk-makt/

development seen in cities like San Francisco, where many travel up to several hours each day to get to work (Dougherty & Burton, 2017).

Gentrification theory posits that when artists and the creative class move in, this contributes to increasing prices in affordable areas (Glass, 1964). Neil Smith (1979) launched a competing theory hypothesizing that gentrification happens due to the rent gap—i.e., potential profit for developers by buying up property in low-income areas with expectation of future gain. Lees et al. (2016) further argued that public organizations also contribute to gentrification with their investments in infrastructure, such as subways, trains, upgrading buildings, and parks. Bringing these three gentrification theories together, we can say that developers, public investments, and the demand for new trendy living areas can drive rent and housing prices, and displace former residents.

Gentrification has spread globally (Glass, 1964) since Glass coined the concept. Examples of areas that have been gentrified include the Latin Quarter in Paris, Prenzlauer Berg in Berlin, and Grünerløkka in Oslo. The changes, as described by gentrification theory, began with the global economic crisis in 1973 and the neoliberal turn that followed, which marked the shift towards a free market and the weakening of the state. States cut their economic transfers to municipalities and industrial production was moved to low-cost countries. This meant, for many cities, a loss of revenue and jobs, which had to be compensated by marketing themselves to attract investments and attractive wage earners (Huse, 2011).

As a consequence of lower state transfers and market orientation, many cities adopted an entrepreneurial form of city policy (Huse, 2011). Richard Florida (2012) described how cities attract the creative class, such as IT consultants, designers, and other high-paid wage earners, to generate economic growth. His book had enormous influence and has led to several cities building opera houses and investing in culture for corporate headquarters and attractive workers to move there. In this sense, Richard Florida can be said to have contributed to the phenomenon of gentrification. For example, the growth and densification of Lillestrøm, a medium-sized Norwegian city near Oslo, is attributed to the emergence of knowledge-intensive businesses, research, a new cultural centre and library that attracted capital, and state investments like the airport shuttle (Lundgaard, 2023).

Tokenism in Urban and Local Community Development

The participation and involvement of citizens has been identified as the solution to generate more interest in local democracy (Hagen et al., 2021; Ruano & Reichborn-Kjennerud, 2022). Still, many experience participation as tokenism, which could be inviting residents to express their opinions on less important matters, or inviting participation in a way that requires disproportionate use of time and expertise that ordinary citizens—especially less resourceful ones—do not have. Usually, the big and important decisions have already been made, while it is precisely these decisions about how the local environment should be developed that residents are interested in having a say in (Legard et al., 2021).

Residents have great expertise about the places they live in. If planners had drawn more on this knowledge, this could have contributed to better places. More is needed than just offering the opportunity to comment on plans presented in ongoing hearing processes. We must also incorporate concrete actions to understand and include the residents in planning. At the same time, politicians should safeguard holistic area planning and focus on community development. A vision for a sustainable community and society development is lacking in these technical processes of urban development. Participation can quickly become a box-ticking exercise that allows politicians to relinquish visions for the common good, instead delegating the task to technocratic participation apparatuses. As a result, no one takes responsibility for the whole—i.e., for social sustainability. It is therefore not enough to argue for better or more participation. Many developers use participation strategically early in the planning phase to get political approval for their plans, which are difficult to understand—for politicians too—and the way residents are included in the planning process is not thorough enough. However, one can ask whether more thorough, better, and more involvement and participation would actually solve the situation, because the question remains: Who is it that should take political responsibility for a positive vision, a comprehensive socially sustainable urban development, and its implementation?

Participation today depends on the goodwill of developers to take residents' wishes and needs into consideration when building, while politicians assume that developers' goodwill will solve the problem. Politicians are too easily convinced by the technical expertise of entrepreneurs in the absence of larger vision for the community or ability and resources to translate visions into reality. In practice, neighborhoods and residents must turn to private companies for cooperation if they are to have any real influence in urban and local community development. Our interviews during the EdiCitNet project[4] in Linderud, Bjerke District, one of the poorest areas in Norway, uncovered that this area lacks meeting places. Most green places are private and belong to housing cooperatives. There is no opportunity to stay there for those who do not live there. The Linderud local community garden, which was erected through the EdiCitNet project, established a new meeting place at the Linderud farm. Therefore, the Linderud community garden became a new outdoor space for the district, which the local population appreciated very much. Seven acres of land were cultivated, and benches and nature paths were laid out around and through the field.[5]

To get a comprehensive grip on development and secure more and better meeting places and public spaces, the district had to approach the contractors directly to try to ensure this more comprehensive development in areas they are responsible for. The DEMUDIG project demonstrated how residents, municipal employees, and politicians navigated within such a system and found that the intentions were good on both sides of the table, as were the frustrations with the situation, since the opportunities to influence the urban development were limited for them.

Residents' Possibility for Participation

Market-driven urban development came as a reaction to changed economic conditions for cities, but it also represented an alternative to the planning traditions from the 1960s that were not always perceived as very successful. This planning tradition was criticized by Jane Jacobs (1961) to be a planning practice that takes too little account of city life as it unfolds on a microscale. She showed how vibrant urban areas function as a social and dynamic organism that takes care of the safety and well-being of those who live there. Because the planners worked in a theoretical universe and planned cities from the top down, they were often not aware of the vibrant city life as it unfolded. They often ended up building living machines that had a destructive effect on social life and cohesion in urban areas (Jacobs,

---

[4] Research project financed by EU's Horizon 2020 Research and Innovation Program. Grant agreement No. 776345. https://www.edicitnet.com/no/hva-er-edicitnet/

[5] https://mia.no/linderud/narmiljohage

1961). Patsy Healy, who is a planner herself, pointed out that this is still the problem under the neoliberal governance regime (Healy, 2007). Few take into account, or bring in residents' interests or knowledge in planning. The problem now is sectoral fragmentation and lack of an overall strategy. A one-sided focus on cities' ability to attract capital does not create good cities to live in, and prioritizing economic surplus does not take into account important values, such as fair distribution of wealth, quality of life, or the environment.

Several researchers have focused on quality of life and better living areas through the UN's concept of social sustainability, in which lies an interest in preserving the needs of the existing residents in central urban areas and preventing gentrification. However, the economic interests and focus on smart cities, where technology is supposed to solve sustainability challenges by building denser and using technology smarter, often stand in opposition to the consideration for good living conditions for existing and new residents, but also for society and citizens in general, as it lacks a focus on social sustainability. Both residents and visitors feel the consequences of suboptimal urban development. In urban areas guided by densification policies, however, property values increase at the same time as the living conditions in the city come under pressure. The development is driven by opportunities for profit, while no one appears to take responsibility for the commons and the living conditions of local communities. Gro Sandkjær Hanssen et al. (2015) focused on this dilemma, showing in detail how the commons is under pressure from densification policy, with reduced access to recreational areas and larger groups exposed to noise and pollution.

Fimreite and Medalen further showed how the public sector's increased cooperation with businesses and civil society has reduced the power of politicians (Fimreite & Medalen, 2005). This happened both through the fragmentation of decision-making in city politics and through more decisions made behind closed doors, further decreasing confidence and trust in electoral democracy. Market orientation has thus become a direct challenge for democracy, as citizens may not feel that voting makes any difference or gives them influence. Their book concludes with a negative scenario, arguing that people must be given greater formal rights to participate and influence, otherwise the negative spiral will continue. Planners must also take into account the time residents have available for participation so that it does not wear people out. The result is otherwise that professionals and capital are the only ones being heard and, in practice, take over urban development (Fimreite & Medalen, 2005).

Participation has been launched as the solution for this lack of democracy in urban development, but it is not clear whether this helps in the context of profound power imbalances between the parties. It is very time-consuming for residents to participate, and they need high competence to do so effectively. Who has the time, resources, and power to participate? Moreover, 80–90% of municipal employees and politicians in Oslo municipality report that participation helps them understand residents' experiences better and gives them a better basis for decision-making, but only 20% of residents report that the municipality's channels for participation give them actual influence. Over twice as many believe that they can gain influence by talking directly to politicians and the administration in the municipality (Legard et al., 2021).

The DEMUDIG project documented that some Norwegian highly-educated and resourceful people who are knowledgeable of the way public planning is organized feel that they have influence on politics. They spend a lot of time and work on several fronts, via the municipality's digital and traditional channels for participation, but also through their own channels, such as social media, newspapers, and television. What they experience as most effective is direct contact with municipal politicians and employees. Few feel that channels set up by the municipality to invite participation and influence give influence on their own. Therefore, the way participation and involvement is organized appears as tokenist (Reichborn-Kjennerud et al. 2021).

Many see participation as a way to promote social sustainability, but we are by no means close to the ideal of real participation (Dokk Holm, 2021). Participation initiatives are far too small and controlled, with limited range and value (Dokk Holm, 2021; Reichborn-Kjennerud et al. 2021). Superusers with high competence, a large network, and a lot of time on their hands succeed to the greatest extent in influencing the important decisions in an area. Digital participation tools have not, to any significant extent, contributed to more democracy and participation, but is an additional arena that needs mastery (Hovik et al., 2022a, 2022b). Residents must spread their time and energy on all available arenas to be heard.

According to the DEMUDIG project survey, those who actually experienced having influence were the enthusiasts working on behalf of their community. They spend a lot of time building networks and competence to influence the development in their local area. When the enthusiasts use their time for the community, it is not a democratic problem, but it can become an issue if individuals who are effective at influencing and who work for special groups' self-interests consistently have more impact than others. This becomes exacerbated if the city is segregated so that resourceful people only work for good urban development where they themselves live. These resident representatives use their free time for advocacy work, while professionals lobby for influence in paid positions. Therefore, a sustainable urban development cannot be based solely on participation and involvement. Politicians must also weigh different considerations and arguments to safeguard a sustainable urban development and take responsibility on behalf of all those who do not have the time or resources to participate, but have placed their trust in elected representatives (Reichborn-Kjennerud et al. 2021).

In this chapter, we initially asked what opportunities residents have to influence their local environment. The answer is that the system does not provide for real co-determination. Participating is time-consuming and requires expertise in how the planning system works. Negotiated contracts often represent barriers to participation and residents are not involved early enough to influence decisions. There is an imbalance in the fact that professionals advocate from paid positions while residents are required to use their free time. In the next chapter, we see what consequences such conditions have on managing cities in a sustainable direction.

References

Amin, A. (2008). Collective culture and urban public space. *City, 12*(1), 5–24.
Amin, A., & Thrift, N. (2002). *Cities: Reimagining the urban*. Polity Press.
Andersen, B., & Røe, P. G. (2017). The social context and politics of large scale urban architecture: Investigating the design of Barcode, Oslo. *European Urban and Regional Studies, 24*(3), 304–317.
Busch, T., Johnsen, E., Vanebo, J. O., & Klausen, K. K. (Eds.). (2004). *Modernisering av offentlig sektor: New Public Management i praksis*. Universitetsforlaget.
Dahlgren, K., Linderud, T., & Schreiner, K. (2021). *Forankring fryder: En bok om medvirkning i byutvikling og arkitektur*. Universitetsforlaget.
Dokk Holm, E. (2021). Lengselen etter å delta. i Dahlgren, K., Linderud, T. & Schreiner, K. (red) Forankring fryder: En bok om medvirkning i byutvikling og arkitektur (pp. 35–47). Universitetsforlaget.
Dougherty, C., & Burton, A. (2017). A 2:15 Alarm, 2 trains and a bus get her to work by 7 A.M. *New York Times*, 17 August 2017. https://www.nytimes.com/2017/08/17/business/economy/san-francisco-commute.html

Dwyer, K. (2022). Don't worry, we're not actually monitoring your productivity. *New York Times*, 19 August 2022. https://www.nytimes.com/2022/08/19/insider/productivity-tracker.html

Falkum, E., Nordrik, B., Wathne, C. T., Drange, I., Hansen, P. B., Dahl, E. M., Kuldova, T., & Underthun, A. (2022). Måling og styring av arbeidstid– Medbestemmelsesbarometeret 2021. AFI-rapport 2022, 01.

Fimreite, A. L., & Medalen, T. (Eds.). (2005). *Governance i norske storbyer: mellom offentlig styring og privat initiativ.* Spartacus.

Florida, R. L. (2012). *The rise of the creative class: Revisited.* Basic Books.

Foucault, M. (1975). Surveiller et punir. Naissance de la prison. Editions Gallimard.

Glass, R. (1964). London: Aspects of change (No. 3). MacGibbon & Kee.

Grund, J. (2019). *Mål og resultatstyring–balansens kunst.* Arbeidsgiverorganisasjonen Spekter.

Hagen, A. L., Andersen, B., Alves, D. E., Brattbakk, I., Dalseide, A. M., Engerbakk, B. B., Hjorth, K., Lorenzen, S. B., Rosten, M. G., Tolstad, I. T., & Vestby, N. (2021). *Ung medvirkning: Kreativitet og konflikt i planlegging.* Nordic Open Access Scholarly Publishing.

Hanssen, G. S. (2013). Medvirkning–med virkning? *Plan, 45*(3), 18–23.

Hanssen, G. S., Hofstad, H., & Saglie, I. L. (Eds.). (2015). *Kompakt byutvikling. Muligheter og utfordringer.* Universitetsforlaget.

Hari, J. (2020). *Lost connections.* Bloomsbury Publishing.

Healy, P. (2007). *Urban complexity and spatial strategies: Towards a relational planning for our times.* Routledge.

Hermansen, T. (2013). Ble det en bedre stat? *Stat & Styring, 23*(2), 24–25. https://doi.org/10.18261/ISSN0809-750X-2013-02-10

Hovik, S., Giannoumis, G. A., Reichborn-Kjennerud, K., Ruano, J. M., McShane, I., & Legard, S. (2022a). *Citizen participation in the information society: Comparing participatory channels in urban development.* Springer Nature.

Huse, T. (2011). *Tøyengata: et nyrikt stykke Norge.* Flamme.

Innset, O. (2020). *Markedsvendingen: Nyliberalismens historie i Norge.* Fagbokforlaget.

Jacobs, J. (1961). *The death and life of great American cities.* Random House.

Kuldova, T., Drange, I., Enehaug, H., Falkum E., Underthun, A., & Wathne, C. T. (2020). Faglig skjønn under press: Fire case-studier og en sammenfatning. AFI Rapport 2020, 06.

Kuldova, T. Ø. (2022). *Compliance-industrial complex: The operating system of a pre-crime society.* Palgrave Pivot. https://doi.org/10.1007/978-3-031-19224-1

Lees, L., Shin, H. B., & López-Morales, E. (2016). *Planetary gentrification.* John Wiley & Sons.

Legard, S., McShane, I., & Ruano, J. M. (2022). What explains the degree of e-participation? A comparison of the adoption of digital participation platforms in Oslo, Melbourne and Madrid. *Information Polity, 28*(3), 359–375.

Legard, S., Reichborn-Kjennerud, K., & Skodvin, A. E. (2021). Medvirkning og påvirkning i Oslos byutvikling. In K. Dahlgren, T. Linderud, & K. Schreiner (Eds.), *Forankring fryder: En bok om medvirkning i byutvikling og arkitektur* (pp. 94–110). Universitetsforlaget.

Linder, J., Voxted, S., Østergaard, M., Michelsen, J., Michelsen, E. B., Schloss, J., Thykjær, C., Sløk, C., Ejler, N., Langenge, M. M., & Linder, A. (2018). *New Public Management i Danmark-baggrund, erfaringer, fremtid*. Dafolo.

Lundgaard, H. (2023). Lillestrøm—suksesshistorie eller voksesyke? Aftenposten, 4 June 2023. https://www.aftenposten.no/norge/i/VPkvr3/lillestroem-suksesshistorie-eller-voksesyke

Mitchell, D. (2003). *The right to the city: Social justice and the fight for public space*. Guilford Press.

Nordahl, B., Barlindhaug, R., & Ruud, M. E. (2008). *Markedsbasert utbyggingspolitikk. Møte mellom kommune og utbygger i pressområder, Samarbeidsrapport*. Norsk institutt for by- og regionsforskning. https://kudos.dfo.no/documents/9135/files/9036.pdf

Piketty, T. (2014). *Capital in the twenty-first century*. Harvard University Press.

Raymen, T. (2015). Designing-in crime by designing-out the social: Situational crime prevention and the intensification of harmful subjectivities. *The British Journal of Criminology, 56*(3), 497–514.

Reichborn-Kjennerud, K. (2016). Politikerne må kjempe for en mindre delt by, Aftenposten, 6 October 2016. https://www.aftenposten.no/meninger/debatt/i/BBP8v/politikerne-maa-kjempe-for-en-mindre-delt-by-kristin-reichborn-kjennerud

Reichborn-Kjennerud, K., de la Fuente, J. R., & Sorando, D. (2021a). Ways to gain influence for residents in two gentrifying neighborhoods: A comparison between Tøyen in Oslo and Lavapiés in Madrid. *Papeles de Población, 27*(110), 109–137. https://rppoblacion.uaemex.mx/article/view/16158

Reichborn-Kjennerud, K., McShane, I., Middha, B., & Ruano, J. M. (2021b). Exploring the relationship between trust and participatory processes: Participation in urban development in Oslo, Madrid and Melbourne. *Nordic Journal of Urban Studies, 1*(2), 94–112.

Rose, N. (1999). *Governing the soul: The shaping of the private self*. Free Association Books.

Ruano, J. M., & Reichborn-Kjennerud, K. (2022). Inside the black box: Perspectives and attitudes of civil servants on citizen participation. In S. Hovik, A. Giannoumis, K. Reichborn-Kjennerud, J. M. Ruano, I. McShane, & S. Legard (Eds.), *Citizen participation in the information society* (pp. 71–95). Palgrave Macmillan.

Sæter, O., & Ruud, M. E. (2005). Byen som symbolsk rom: bypolitikk, stedsdiskurser og gentrifisering i Gamle Oslo.

Sennett, R. (2005). Capitalism and the city: Globalization, flexibility, and indifference. In Y. Kazepow (Ed.), *Cities of Europe: Changing contexts, local arrangements, and the challenge to urban cohesion* (pp. 109–122). Blackwell Publishing.

Smith, N. (1979). Toward a theory of gentrification a back to the city movement by capital, not people. *Journal of the American Planning Association*, 45(4), 538–548.

Sørgjerd, C. (2018). I omstridte byggesaker går byrådet til FRP og Høyre for å få flertall. Aftenposten, 9 July 2018. https://www.aftenposten.no/oslo/i/bK2ogA/i-omstridte-byggesaker-gaar-byraadet-til-frp-og-hoeyre-for-aa-faa-flertall

Veggeland, N. (2009). *Taming the regulatory state: Politics and ethics.* Edward Elgar Publishing Ltd..

Veggeland, N. (2010). *Den nye reguleringsstaten: Idébrytinger og styringskonflikter.* Gyldendal Akademisk.

Voldnes, F. (2012a). Folkevalgt styring eller markedsstyring? *Samfunn og økonomi*, 2, 6–27.

Voldnes, F. (2012b). Markedsretting av offentlig sektor: Virkemidler og alternativer. Fagforbundet. https://assets-global.website-files.com/65e884f8fffb6d610d77c46d/65fc3739f69e601b3352005b_Markedsretting%20des%202012.pdf

CHAPTER 6

The Sustainable City: Barriers and Enablers

Abstract Globally, an increasing number of people are moving to cities. The United Nations therefore believes that the solution to the climate crisis must be found in their governance and organization. Nevertheless, the prioritization of compact urban development in cities comes at the expense of some of the values in social and environmental sustainability. This chapter presents a model on who has power to influence city development, taking account of three dimensions: the social, material, and discursive. The chapter uses the District of Tøyen in Oslo as an example to demonstrate how these dimensions play out in a concrete central city district. Developers have most influence both in planning and building the city, but they have little interest in letting citizens participate. Green areas and the commons are hard to prioritize, as property prices increase, making the city less affordable for normal wage earners to live in.

Keywords UN • Social sustainability • Discursive space • Material space • Social space • Social capital

Globally, an increasing number of people are moving to cities. The United Nations (UN) therefore believes that the solution to the climate crisis must be found in their governance and organization. Most people live in cities, creating a need to plan more sustainable cities. The compact city

© The Author(s), under exclusive license to Springer Nature Switzerland AG 2025
K. Reichborn-Kjennerud, *Sustainable Urban Transitions and New Public Management*,
https://doi.org/10.1007/978-3-031-82307-7_6

with short distances between the places people live, their workplaces, and service offerings is an ideal that provides a basis for sustainable mobility that reduces CO_2 emissions. Norway has embraced compact urban development with emphasis on high land use around public transport hubs as a core planning principle. However, parallel to this development, we also see, as aforementioned, the costs of this development: more pressure on the commons. Environmental and social sustainability for residents in dense cities is thereby challenged (Hanssen et al., 2015), and pressure on existing residential areas and conflicts seem to escalate.

Social sustainability includes residents' subjective experiences of their living environment. Additionally, social capital, participation, and networks, reciprocity, and trust between neighbors are included in the concept of social sustainability. The prioritization of compact urban development often comes at the expense of these social values. Therefore, residents should, to a greater extent, be considered a resource in planning to increase the quality of areas, because they have local knowledge about what the population needs and what is perceived as important (Hanssen et al., 2015). Environmental sustainability is not just about reducing greenhouse gas emissions, but also preserving biodiversity and the impact green areas have on residents' living conditions, health, and air quality (Hanssen et al., 2015).

Several aspects affect the social sustainability of a city. The qualities of the physical surroundings, residents' opportunities for participation, and the narratives about the city are some of the most central factors, and are closely interwoven. It is important for residents to have networks enabling them to secure their democratic rights. With cooperation and good networks, they can more effectively fight gentrification and protect local parks and other commons in their area. As for their physical surroundings, capital interests in the smart city often conflict with those of residents. For instance, some residents have an interest in price increases if they own their own apartment, but most who wish to continue living in an area experience the pressure on meeting places, green areas, and the commons as negative. The rent gap in gentrifying areas provides profit opportunities for developers, and it is most profitable for them to build as densely as possible. The narratives, or discourses, about the city have consequences in their own right both in the social and material space. If an area is positively mentioned in newspapers and social media, it can attract buyers and investors to the area. Conversely, an area can be stigmatized if it is described as dangerous and unattractive. Those who have the power to influence these spaces of the social, material, and discursive have power in urban development.

The model below illustrates how social sustainability is maintained (or not) in social and material spaces, and the narratives about them. The way these three dimensions interconnect has implications for power and influence in urban development.

Model of Power and Influence in Urban Development

In the material space, financial strength and the ability to influence regulation and processes are important power factors. Developers, property owners, investors, and those who can afford to buy and rent have power. The material space highlights how changes in the physical structures of an area occur. Those who have control over the physical structures are typically property owners, developers, and affluent individuals who can buy, rent, and renovate property. The municipality and state organizations that can regulate, invest, and upgrade buildings and physical infrastructure, as well as enthusiasts and smaller or larger businesses trying to influence urban development in a resident-friendly direction, can also have power. The material space can affect the social space—i.e., building too many one-room apartments makes it hard for families to stay.

In the social space, collaboration in groups and networks gives power. A common term for this phenomenon is social capital, which is central to social sustainability. Through cooperation and contacts with people who have power and influence, residents can gain power to influence urban development. The social space is about how residents in an area collaborate to make their neighborhood a better place to live. For example, enthusiasts can organize people around specific issues and interests, and involve key people with contacts in politics and media who help influence more effectively. People can also build social capital through voluntary activities in an area. The social space can influence the material space through neighborhood groups pushing for parks, alternative housing forms, and other social initiatives that benefit residents. Both Robert Putnam (2015) and Pierre Bourdieu (1995) have described the concept of social capital in different ways.

The narratives about an area, or the discursive space, is about the way we talk about neighborhoods in various channels. Do we talk the areas up or down, and within which frameworks of understanding do we communicate? Those who have power in the discursive space often have high cultural, social, and economic capital (Bourdieu, 1995). They are articulate and get their arguments heard in various arenas, which could be public debate or more closed fora that those with high cultural capital have better access to than people with lower cultural and economic capital (Bourdieu, 1995). In the discursive space, residents who master various communication platforms in mass and social media use these channels to influence. Public authorities' formal digital platforms can also be used to gain influence in urban development, and Tte discursive space can interact with the two other spaces through the creation of meaning. The discourse about an area can influence the material space by talking the prices up or down, and can also influence the social space. For example, local residents can become proud of their area, or feel stigmatized, by the way their neighborhood is talked about in the media. The discourse about areas influences what actually happens there. An example is whether people choose to buy an apartment in a neighborhood or not, or go on a Sunday walk there. In urban analyses, it is therefore useful to also emphasize the meaning aspects of the city. How do we read the urban space and how do we talk about the city? What opinions do we attribute to what we see? The manner in which we talk and write about areas in the city communicates in certain ways what residents and inhabitants interpret. Narratives about the city function as knowledge frames—ways of thinking or writing about a topic, a kind of codified knowledge. All statements operate within a codified discourse (Pløger, 2002), which today often takes place digitally, in newspapers, and social media. There is also an internal discourse in digital professional and administrative systems in public organizations.

The semiologist Roland Barthes believed that we must read the city's signs (Barthes, 1991; Reichborn-Kjennerud, 1997). The city can be read as a text through socio-spatial symbols, which become a form of communication system. Representations are socially constructed, both in their production and in the way they are received and interpreted. Hence, they can be constructed in different ways with different outcomes. Trendy coffee bars and galleries can be read as hip and innovative, a sort of environment where Richard Florida's creative class would thrive (Florida, 2012), but the same areas can also be read as places for capital accumulation, where the less hip and resourceful are priced out and pushed to the city's outskirts.

Language has the power to motivate and change. As cities have moved from an industrial to a communication and consumer society, they no longer primarily manufacture goods, but rather symbols, which can be read as a text and discourse. Factories in the West are emptied of workers and transformed into art halls, which produce symbols, logos, and advertising texts, while production takes place in low-cost countries, often under exploitative working conditions. Cities become hubs in a globalized economy, vying to attract economic activity by using symbols. The city itself becomes a cultural product: city branding (Dinnie, 2011). It is the symbolic aspects of a neighborhood that attract both investors and groups of residents (Zukin, 2012). All these spaces influence social sustainability. Examples from the DEMUDIG project show how this either hinders or promotes a socially sustainable development, and which logics become visible.

URBAN GOVERNANCE

The market reforms introduced as of the 1980s were meant to improve efficiency, but instead increased the number of bureaucrats in the Norwegian public service. In municipalities today, we find a mix of the traditional bureaucracy (OPM) and New Public Management (NPM). These are characterized by silo-structured specialist units for individual services. They combine Management by Objectives and Results (MBOR) and strict cost control with an inward professional focus. We do not see less, but another type of regulation after market reforms (Hermansen, 2013; Innset, 2020). All economic policy, including the neoliberal *laissez-faire* policy, requires some form of regulation. Laws and regulations are legal constructions that make new markets possible (Pistor, 2019). Therefore, the question is not whether the credit and housing sectors were regulated or not, but how they were regulated: from a governance anchored in democratic processes that sought to achieve specific political goals to a form of market regulation that was supposed to ensure maximum growth and efficiency. The latter reforms put politicians at arm's length from the sectors, but at the same time, weakened the democratic control of society (Innset, 2020). It is great if the public sector can deliver services efficiently by changing the control and management of its organizations, but it should not do so without responsiveness to citizens (Sintomer et al., 2008).

The aforementioned Norwegian *Planning and Building Act* of 2008 does not, in itself, represent an obstacle to sustainable planning. It has been evaluated and considered a good and modern tool for sustainable development and public health work (Hofstad 2018). In the Act, sustainability is the very intention of planning, and sustainable development is one of the most important purposes. The law has been evaluated, and appears modern and in line with international development led by the adoption of the UN's 17 sustainability goals (Hanssen & Aarsæther, 2018).

Health-promoting local communities, sense of belonging, social capital, and participation are four of seven considerations that should be addressed within the social sustainability dimension, and which are important in a planning context. The last three are linked to basic needs that ensure quality of life, well-being, cohesion, and justice. These aspects are relevant for public health work. The social sustainability dimension is, however, the one least understood in planning (Hanssen & Aarsæther, 2018). The means to achieve the social goals can, at the same time, be encompassed within several of the other sustainability dimensions.

In the evaluation of the *Planning and Building Act* of 2008, the planning managers in the municipalities reported that economic and environmental sustainability is much better taken care of than the social. The planning managers experienced social sustainability as difficult to understand and challenging to implement. They also perceived it as difficult to measure, ambiguous, and diffuse. The responses from the evaluation suggest that municipalities have not made any radical changes. They govern according to short-term economic parameters and take environmental considerations when they do not conflict with economic return. Environmental considerations, such as soil conservation, are under pressure, while densification and construction of a high number of centrally-located compact homes are embraced, often at the expense of the quality of the homes (Hofstad, 2018). The responses also suggest that social sustainability is perceived as too complex and difficult to understand by planning managers. At the same time, the power and strength of the sustainability concept lies precisely in its complexity. It is by taking into account complexity that we can achieve a real transformation of systems, as it is about being visionary and operational on a strategic level. This, in turn, involves creative exploration of new ways of planning. MBOR cannot help tap into the potential of sustainable development (Hofstad, 2018).

It is important to know resident needs and challenges well before implementing measures. Therefore, the planner could conduct research to find out what these challenges are, for example, through the use of site analysis (Hanssen, 2021). Residents and the area must be placed at the centre of this work because the problem should be seen from the perspective of those who will actually use the area. It is important to work interdisciplinary between departments and organizations.

Today, the urban development in Norway is market-driven and neoliberal. A more comprehensive and long-term social planning system may require a public sector that thinks in a more urban sociological, anthropological, and geographical perspective. In a geographically delimited area, everything is relevant to consider, from rocks and wildlife, to transport and the composition of the local population. This is why urban studies have been questioned as a subject, because it is difficult to define and delimit. However, in a society where sustainability guides planning, the authorities need to think more comprehensively about everything from bird life to the inclusion of residents. Hence, the municipality must ask what is in the bird's interest and then take its perspective. Similarly, it must ask what is in the child's interest and then take the child's perspective. Ask the child or the pensioner what they want in their local environment. Have an interest in what birds, animals, nature and the people who live in an area want (Sachs Olsen, 2021). People need not only a number of services of various kinds or a number of homes and schools, so the municipality should take an ethnographic, qualitative approach to what provides good living conditions for residents in a local area—i.e., understand people's subjective experiences and use that as a central source of knowledge. This could lead to real co-creation. Research surveys and site analyses designed to help the municipality understand a local area better before measures are implemented could also be used as methods for real participation (Reichborn-Kjennerud & Ophaug, 2018). Therefore, the challenge is to adopt a more open starting point and to try out different solutions to create good living conditions, and perhaps think more in a site-based way in social planning. Important questions to ask are: What can make places more open and inclusive? What can make them interesting? What can draw people to places where they can meet other people and positively impact the environment? Safeguarding fertile ground for social entrepreneurs and non-profit organizations is, for example, a way to create value and solve more than one challenge at a time. Development takes time, and not all results are equally easy to measure, particularly not in the short-term. Some initiatives can be the start of a positive development for an individual, community, or an area over a somewhat longer time period.

Influencing Urban Development: The Social Space

How can residents influence urban development and when do they take the trouble to get involved? If residents in an area feel that urban development is harming their local environment, they often protest, and if they manage to fight for their interests in an effective way, this is described as high social capital—a term used, in social research, for civil society's ability to develop trustful relationships between citizens, and thus strengthen the community's ability to solve collective problems and challenges (Putnam, 2015).

Social capital can bind individuals together as a specific homogeneous group. It can be a religious group or a fan club for a football team. Alternatively, social capital can help build trust between citizens from different social strata and cultural environments. It is primarily the latter type of social capital that has significance for social integration and democracy in a modern large-scale and complex society. The most commonly used understanding of the term, linked to the work of American political scientist Robert D. Putnam, is "a local community's ability to build trust, common norms, and networks, which will make it easier to achieve coordinated actions and thus improve the efficiency of society." This type of social capital is often investigated by measuring the level of trust in the population. Analyses by Putnam showed that the social capital within each region had a clear positive effect on the functioning of local democracy (Putnam, 1993). High social capital contributed to better local democracy and more efficient service delivery. In Putnam's work, social capital is used to describe residents' ability to develop trustful relationships, so that they acquire a better ability, as a community, to solve collective problems and challenges. When they come into contact with each other, the residents start to cooperate to make their area a better place. Putnam also showed how these social local structures are eroding in the US, as social capital decreases when everyone bowls alone and no longer engages in local organizations (Putnam, 2015).

Pierre Bourdieu's concept of social capital differs from Putnam's, as the former links the concept to an analysis of social classes and cultural differences. Social capital exists through many different networks and can be converted by individuals into cultural or economic capital. The value of social capital depends on the networks the individuals are part of. Bourdieu can be relevant for our understanding of the way in which people with networks can convert their social capital into more influence in urban development. The DEMUDIG project showed how individuals used high social capital to influence people in their network to safeguard local interests. People with planning competence, knowledge of how the media works, and contacts in local politics fought for the local community's interests, for instance, in the Tøyen area, in an inclusive way.

The terms "bonding, bridging, and linking" are used in recent analyses of area-based initiatives (Agger & Jensen, 2015). Bonding represents relationships between friends and family, people who know each other well and resemble each other, while bridging describes relationships between different types of people who may have more peripheral contact both formally and informally. They have so-called "weak ties" (Granovetter, 1973). However, Agger and Jensen have called for more research on linking, which describes contact that residents in areas with challenging living conditions have with people in power (Agger & Jensen, 2015). The question thus becomes how a strengthened network in an area contributes to influencing people with power in urban development. Bourdieu describes social capital within a social field, as individuals having contacts, and through these being able to influence policy. In areas with challenging living conditions, residents often do not have contact with people in power that could influence urban development. More resourceful people, with these types of contacts and competence to influence, may be positive for the local community's ability to influence policy, and typically move into these areas during the gentrification process. These residents have the desire to contribute to improvements in their local area, and if they can influence urban development policy, it can improve the area in general and thus benefit everyone living there, including future residents. Conversely, one could also imagine that the interests of individual groups may conflict with each other, which is also typical for gentrified areas. If residents close a street to traffic to ensure traffic safety for school children, this may go against the interests of the shop owners on the street. Now their customers can no longer drive right up to the shop and profits go down. One can also imagine individuals blocking measures that would otherwise have been of common interest to the area by using the municipality's procedures for complaining.

Not all social capital can be converted into influence in urban development (Linstad, 2018). However, the residents of Tøyen have worked together to promote the neighborhood's interests and social sustainability in the area. The quote below gives an indication of what works, namely using one's network of people with high cultural capital. The Program Office at Tøyen is the municipal organization that represents the area's interests in the area-based initiative. It works to improve living conditions in Tøyen, but does not have a lot of power. However, the network of resourceful enthusiasts working for the interests of the residents of Tøyen is very valuable, as explained by a resident:

> Then there's us, the Tøyen campaign and the network of journalists, writers and people who are in contact with or in networks with people in power. They can set the agenda and are good at using the media. The Program Office has little to no power. They are a secretariat with a high turnover.

Hence, residents with resourceful contacts contribute to safeguarding residents' interests in the area and to social sustainability. However, the fact that cohesion in a district is perceived as good is not always enough to create positive development in the local environment. A quote from a resident shows how the system can be experienced as frustrating, despite good cohesion in the area:

> Participation and influence are empty words. We persevere as long as we have good neighbors. But there are limits to everything.

Municipal regulation and developers' priorities influence the material space, and both can contribute to putting pressure on an area's social sustainability. For example, it is easier for developers to sell small apartments. When municipal authorities allow them to build mostly small apartments, it reduces the possibility for a diverse neighborhood where families can continue to stay when the children grow older and need more space. As a resident expressed:

> The cohesion between permanent residents in the district is exceptionally good, but we constantly experience (…) buildings (…) being converted from family apartments to small one room apartments. This increases the turnover in the district.

The material space can also put pressure on social sustainability through market-oriented regulations. Voluntary organizations and smaller independent shops and eateries quickly lose out when the municipality charges large fees for rezoning and change of use. Such regulations can contribute to the emergence of larger chain stores with financial muscle at the expense of smaller independent shops, eateries, and non-profit organizations. The larger players often have better administrative capacity and financial ability to pay. When non-profit organizations and smaller businesses are displaced through such processes, residents' needs are poorly met. As one resident expressed:

> Is it right that a non-profit association working to improve outdoor activities is forced to carry out a costly and uncertain regulation process to improve a ski trail through bureaucratic processes that drive up the costs for the association to the unmanageable?

The same frustration was felt by a resident in another district when large fees were demanded for the change of use of a small shop:

> Is it right that a change of use from shop to serving in order to stimulate life in the city should take years and cost a small independent store several hundred thousand Norwegian Kroner?

Based on the frustrated statements of residents in central districts, one can ask whether the residents still trust that municipal authorities take care of the interests of the local community. If residents feel that they are not being heard and that local considerations are not taken into account, it can have negative effects on trust in the authorities. However, how do resident representatives actually work to stop initiatives they believe will harm the neighborhood, or what do they do to have measures implemented they believe will benefit the area, such as building a sports hall for children and young people?

How Resident Representatives Work to Promote their Interests

According to the DEMUDIG research project, the most effective way to influence urban development is to directly contact municipal employees at the town hall level, municipal agencies, the district's administration, or to talk directly to politicians. Raising issues in district councils and city council committees is also a good strategy. Representatives in the urban development committee often make their own city council group aware of cases they think are important and can also follow-up and check the status of cases. Personal meetings with residents influence politicians' priorities, and the latter respect genuine engagement in the population, especially with regards to initiatives not raised by special interest groups' interests only, but with groups that aim to include everyone. Over time, persistence is often a prerequisite for success in influencing policy. Still, developers have the greatest power to influence city development, even though resident and sports associations can successfully influence in individual cases.

The municipality's own participation channels do not give residents any influence to speak of. Politicians and municipal employees confirm residents' own experience that it is hard to influence urban development through the municipality's channels. Residents' blogs and websites provide more influence than using the municipality's participatory channels. The media getting involved, asking questions, and demanding the politicians step up in specific cases can be very effective. Mobilizing networks of architects and landscape architects, who can spread alternative proposals and suggestions on social media, inviting city councillors to specific places to see and understand the consequences of decisions, and holding them accountable are also effective strategies.

Effective mobilization in networks and visibility in the media help, as well as contacts with people in power. It is smart to involve journalists, writers, and people who are good at using the media. The Tøyen Campaign, which arranges local activities, and the Tøyen Initiative, which fights to improve living conditions, conditions for children, and participation in the Tøyen area, are examples of this. The Tøyen Initiative collaborates with a diversity of actors across cultures, religions, and social backgrounds. People involved in the Tøyen Initiative understand the game of the media as well as the political one and have made the Tøyen Village a concept. Thus, they have been good at using the media and politicians to push their agenda.

Nine out of 10 politicians and municipal employees believe that participation from residents is important, and provides increased understanding and a better decision-making basis. However, residents still do not feel heard. The majority believe urban development is unfair and that it is not handled correctly. It is a paradox that everyone seems to be positive about participation, but to actually implement participation in a good way seems challenging.

Findings from the DEMUDIG project showed that resident representatives must use several channels to influence, and that they must engage often and over time to be heard (Reichborn-Kjennerud et al., 2021). Participation and involvement in urban development processes thus become very time-consuming and working effectively to influence also requires specific competence and knowledge.

Good social cohesion in a district is not sufficient to safeguard residents' interests. It is necessary to also have a strong network position. Social capital must be converted into cultural and economic capital to translate into influence in urban development. Cultural capital is necessary for setting the agenda and leveraging discourse in the media and social media, but it is also crucial to use a network of opinion leaders and resourceful persons who know politicians and administrators high up in the system. One must use a combination of several channels simultaneously to be heard. Cultural capital is useful in approaching case handlers. Speaking the same language and knowing the administration's system result in greater chances to influence than if you, as a resident representative, provide input that does not meet formal requirements. Addressing your case directly in political committees is also relatively effective. At the same time, resident representatives have little to no power to influence development projects that have already been approved. Residents and politicians feel bound by agreements that have been negotiated by the administration, and residents also become frustrated by processes that take a disproportionately long time even though the proposals apparently concern simple measures, such as getting a 30km/h-zone sign outside a school. It takes a long time to get uncontroversial proposals accepted, but is also difficult to navigate who is responsible for what within the municipality. Residents often spend a lot of time in meetings with people who are not relevant for their case.

In central city districts, business interests, the interests of visitors from within the city, and of visitors from outside often conflict with the interests of those that live in the area. A problem in many popular southern European tourist cities, including Madrid, is Airbnb, or the fact that apartments are converted into tourist apartments. Airbnb increases living costs for residents and has become a problem. Residents are frustrated that local politicians do not address this adequately. In Oslo, the challenge is more that larger apartments are converted into very small apartments, which increase the turnover in the districts. Renting out homes and splitting larger apartments into smaller units creates instability in an area because more people move in and out. This affects social sustainability negatively. Gentrification affects not only residents, but also smaller business owners that also cannot bear the increasing costs in central areas. Social sustainability is thus negatively affected when the authorities make business-friendly changes in regulatory provisions, and build higher and denser without the neighborhood receiving corresponding upgrades in the outdoor areas that can support and maintain good living conditions. Green spaces in central urban areas are also under pressure from the privatization of areas—i.e., park areas being converted into football fields or kindergartens.

Local groups can fight for improvements in areas and succeed in upgrading their neighborhood. This, in turn, often makes areas more popular, and increased popularity is reflected in higher housing prices, which are an advantage for those who own their own home, but can become a problem for those who rent and have a low income. Hence, gentrification processes are strengthened: the coffee costs more, rent increases, and it becomes too expensive for the local baker to rent. Instead, modern coffee bars and chains establish themselves in the baker's premises, and the fabric store and Asian market also have to move. Expensive clothing stores pop up in their stead. Upgrading can thus have unintended consequences. The intention may have been to make the area a nicer place to live in, but the result becomes an area too expensive for current residents. The development of Grünerløkka in the 1800s and the ship construction site in Vika, which was developed into Aker Brygge at the end of the 1980s, are two examples of areas in Oslo that have fully or partially been gentrified.

This type of development can quickly trigger residents to engage in urban and local community development in their area. The main reasons why residents engage are that they experience the development as a challenge for the neighborhood, and also that they feel they have knowledge and opinions that can help the place. Many are generally politically engaged and believe locals know which development is best. Most of those who engage in urban development are motivated by making the neighborhood better for everyone who lives there. In the DEMUDIG project's survey, significantly fewer said that the reason they contribute is that the urban development initiative can affect them personally. This indicates that most enthusiasts spending time engaging in urban development are unselfishly motivated on behalf of the community. This is, at least, how they think about it themselves. At the same time, one group may strongly disagree with other groups about what is best for the neighborhood. An example is different perceptions of the importance of car accessibility, and juggling these different preferences can be challenging for politicians and municipal employees. However, information about residents' preferences and opinions can still improve solutions, as all information is desirable for good urban development. However, it is a bad idea to open up for participation without actually using the inputs to find better solutions. The experience of not being heard can reduce trust in politicians and local democracy.

Trust is a social glue lubricating all relationships. If individuals and groups trust each other, there is less need for control. Trust is built up over time when those benefitting from the trust deliver what is expected. Those who are trusted must show, in practice, that they deserve the trust. It takes a long time to build up such trust relationships, but they are easy to tear down through one or a few breaches of trust. The DEMUDIG project's survey showed that in Madrid, almost 70% distrusted the politicians in urban development politics. Madrid developed the most radical digital co-determination platform of the three cities (Oslo, Madrid, and Melbourne), maybe as a consequence of this distrust. In Oslo, nearly half of respondents distrusted politicians' urban development policies. An approximately equal number distrusted municipal administrations' implementation of these policies. This may indicate that low trust leads to demands for more co-determination outside of elections. Citizens of Oslo believe in the good intention of politicians, but are less convinced of their ability to steer urban development politics in a resident-friendly direction in practice. Nevertheless, residents in all three cities claim that local politicians have poor knowledge of or lack interest in the areas they govern, and that they are most interested in their own voters and ideological battles with political opponents. Some respondents also believe that politicians listen more to businesses than to residents. Politicians can easily be tempted or pressured to make priorities that do not help the local community, but rather promote capital or business interests. The residents who responded to the DEMUDIG project's survey feel that business interests prevail, while participatory democracy in practice does not help safeguard the interests of the local community. Politicians, on the other hand, have a different perspective on the matter. They have to consider multiple interests and sometimes experience residents confusing the right to express their opinion with the right to determine the outcome. There are thus legitimate arguments from both resident representatives, who do not feel heard, and politicians, who point out that different groups may have different interests in an area and that this also must be taken into account.

Residents are frustrated because they perceive participatory processes as being organized without an intention of letting them influence decisions. They do not just want to provide input to give the municipality a better basis for decision-making, but to influence the way their area should develop. As a resident from Melbourne expressed:

> It's not enough to tick the box for having organized participatory activity. Moreland initiated participation activities, but it's difficult to get them to actively listen. It feels like they have already made up their minds, and are only there to entertain us. Instead of listening they stand by and defend their decisions. It's very alienating and you feel like withdrawing, except that it's where you live and what's at stake is a development that will affect your family.

Trust in Local Politicians in Urban Development

Trust in politicians and municipal employees in Oslo is high compared to Madrid and Melbourne. Residents in Oslo perceive that politicians and municipal employees intend to develop the city in a way that takes into account residents' interests, even though they do not necessarily deliver what residents want (Reichborn-Kjennerud et al., 2021). Residents' own perception of influence significantly impacts their level of trust in politicians and the administration. The same is the case for employees, as documented in *The Co-determination Survey* measuring the state of Norwegian working life democracy (Falkum et al., 2022). When residents or employees feel that they have influence, it leads to higher trust. The reason why higher perceived influence leads to higher trust can both be due to the residents having experienced that the input they provide is taken into account, but also to a historically high level of trust in Norway, where residents generally trust politicians and the bureaucracy, but one could always question whether this trust is deserved. The causal relationship can go both ways—i.e, residents have influence and reason to trust or they perceive that they have more influence than in reality (Reichborn-Kjennerud et al., 2021). Participation in processes is not necessarily the same as actually having real power and influence over decisions.

It must be taken into consideration that representatives of residents in an area do not always represent everyone's interests. Thus, there is a certain risk associated with giving resident representatives decisive influence over decisions. Responses to the DEMUDIG survey suggest that a group of people is very active in influencing urban development policy, while most people engage only occasionally a few times a year. Those who spend the most time on participation trying to influence local community development feel that they gained the most influence. It takes a lot of time to gain influence in urban development policies in Oslo. You must engage at least once a month, but it is only when residents engage every day that they experience having influence in local urban and community development to a large extent. In the other cities, this correlation was not as clear. Nevertheless, the number of arenas and platforms residents engaged in correlated positively with perceived influence (Hovik et al., 2022).

In Norway, municipalities are required to involve actors affected by measures in planning processes. Some methods municipalities can use to involve are holding advisory referenda and delegating decisions to committees. Victoria, the local government for the city of Melbourne, involves residents by consulting with the community about service provision, annual budgets, and government strategies. Spanish municipalities, among the most autonomous in Europe, are required to facilitate citizen involvement politically, socially, economically, and culturally. In many cases, budget decisions have been delegated to local residents. In Norway, there is high support for representative political bodies and public services but this strong support may not have led to pressure on the system towards new ways of involving citizens. In Madrid, innovative solutions for participatory democracy have been most radical and innovative. Madrid also went through a severe economic crisis followed by austerity measures, which, in turn, led to unemployment and eviction of people who could no longer pay their housing loans. This led to lower trust in the authorities and large demonstrations (Legard et al., 2022).

The DEMUDIG survey reached residents who in some way represent organized interests and who spend a lot of time and resources to influence policies. However, the average man or woman on the street is probably less active in trying to influence urban development politics than resident representatives who speak on behalf of their community. For this system to work democratically, these representatives must represent community interests in their area.

A lot of competence is required to be heard in urban development politics, as explained by one of our informants:

> There are big differences in the effectiveness to influence. I'm in a professional position and have knowledge, experience, network, and a platform through my organization. In addition, my organization has financial resources for lobbying. For the groups I collaborate with and partly represent, the situation is different. Many people from these groups are in some way or other partly excluded from societal arenas, which also affects their role as active citizens. They have not been heard, they do not know how to get heard, or they have given up being heard.

Politicians and municipal employees are generally very positive towards participation, even though there are challenges with making participation and involvement work in practice. A majority of politicians and municipal employees think it takes too much time to organize good participatory processes. Most of them acknowledge that the participation processes they organize today are not good enough, and almost everyone sees the danger of citizens losing motivation if they invest a lot of time without seeing results. At the same time, they are worried that participatory democracy does not always contribute to fair decisions as strong groups know how to use the system more effectively. Resourceful people can capture the processes and gain influence at the expense of the silent voices, residents who are rarely seen or heard. Almost all municipal employees stated in the DEMUDIG project that it is difficult to mobilize the silent voices. We saw the same tendency in Madrid and Melbourne. The fact that primarily residents with high levels of education engage raises the question of who looks after the interests of those who do not organize. There is a tendency for those who know how to set the agenda to be effective in influencing, while the rest are passive and not seen.

This way, municipal employees can quickly find themselves in a double bind where they have to protect the common interest from effective influencers. The work situation for municipal employees is further complicated by the fact that people who participate often struggle to distinguish between the right to make proposals and the right to specific results. At the same time, a consultancy market for participation has emerged. Participation is becoming professionalized because it is demanding and takes a lot of time. Organizing participation processes then expands the market for consultancy companies, which reduces authentic engagement between residents and their elected representatives. The professionalization of participation can also obscure the real challenges residents are concerned about.

An additional problem is that municipal employees do not have systems for processing tips and proposals from residents that come via municipal websites, mobile apps, and social media pages. Only 12% of municipal employees in the DEMUDIG survey believed that they have systems for processing residents' proposals, and 30% systematize proposals from residents that come in via their own participatory channels. At the same time, 36% of those surveyed are supposed to set aside time for participation as part of their job description, but the systems they have to support this work are not good enough and are rarely evaluated and improved. As a municipal employee expressed:

> It is a challenge to figure out how to process input that does not necessarily follow the formal requirements, the process requirements, and linguistic jargon of the planning profession, without the input being dismissed as irrelevant. I think many inputs are not followed up sufficiently because people out there do not know the tribal language and practices, and because case handlers have few tools and little time to process input that does not fit the system.

Municipal employees find that they have little opportunity to handle input from residents due to time constraints, the way the administrative processes are set up, and because they cannot promise too much without approval at various management levels. Another important reason is that decisions have sometimes already been made. However, the districts are more focused and responsive to residents than agencies and departments in the municipal organization. The districts often see urban development through the eyes of residents and are more aware of and concerned for their needs.

Politicians and municipal employees clearly expressed, through the DEMUDIG survey, that they are interested in the silent voices' point of view (people who likely do not have as much time and as high competence to influence as their more resourceful counterparts). However, the silent voices are difficult to get in touch with. If this is the case, the way participation and involvement is organized today may need improvement. The DEMUDIG project showed that many realize the need to work differently. A public employee said:

It is important to support grassroots movements and build trust in the groups that need to be heard. This can only be done through long time presence in an area. If this is achieved, and typical silent voices get the opportunity and courage to use their voice, we can get attention to important issues and eventually also make important changes.

With new digital solutions, optimism has increased for the possibility of influencing authorities more effectively, such as through social media, but this is not a method that can replace regular social networking. Social media often becomes a platform for promoting self-interests, so-called Not in My Backyard viewpoints. The DEMUDIG survey revealed some scepticism towards the ability of social media to take the lead in building community in neighborhoods. Compared to face-to-face local engagement and initiatives, social media is more individualistic and not as apt to build cohesion locally. On the other hand, social media can be useful for initiating engagement to build networks. Several Facebook groups have been of great help in individual cases and for connecting people, for example, through buying, selling, and exchanging things locally, which can contribute to social cohesion. Residents also use social media to some extent to encourage dialogue for local problem-solving, to build community values, and connect people in the local community.

Social media is not a replacement for face-to-face meetings in communities. Almost half of those surveyed in the DEMUDIG survey do not use social media to build local networks. Perhaps the enthusiasts that spend a lot of time engaging in local community development build networks and work for the area through social media. However, not all groups use social media, or can effectively do so in advocacy work. Often, personal networks and contacts are more important, at least for certain groups of immigrants. In engaging people, it is also central to assure them that collaboration is non-binding and harmless, and that the purpose of the network is to work against gentrification, include everyone, and retain a mixed population, including the not so well-off.

Cohesion and Co-creation in Neighborhoods

In the DEMUDIG survey, 29% of respondents from the central districts in Oslo said that people in their neighborhood feel like a family to them, but a majority expressed that they do not experience it that way. This may indicate that cohesion in the local community may feel strongest for certain groups. In Oslo, 36% believed that those living in their neighborhood share values, compared to 33% who did not share that opinion. A majority in Madrid's central districts believed that residents do not share values, while 64% in Melbourne believed the residents share values. Therefore, it seems that Melbourne's central districts have the most cohesion. An interesting theory could be that since trust in the municipality and politicians is so low in Melbourne, the inhabitants perceive that they are more dependent on each other than on the public apparatus, while those in Madrid struggle with a combination of pressure from too much tourism, corruption, and low trust, which wears on local cohesion. The survey did not address a representative sample of residents, but was sent to residents' representatives, so these figures must be interpreted with caution.

The cases residents engage with in the central districts of Oslo, Madrid, and Melbourne are similar. The problems reported are largely about pressure on green spaces and the commons, too much densification, conversion of family homes into smaller homes—in turn leading to turnover and a poorer living environment—traffic issues, prioritization of political interests that are not perceived to benefit the district and the residents living there, fragmentation of responsibility, poor responsiveness to local needs from city agencies with responsibilities that affect local urban development, and an impenetrable planning system that does not allow for input from residents. Madrid has the highest pressure on housing prices and most noise as a result of tourism, but the other cities face the same challenges, but to a lesser extent.

However, some neighborhoods have better cohesion and capacity to work for common interests in their area. The District of Old Oslo was one of five downtown districts we collected questionnaire data from. Tøyen, in the District of Gamle Oslo, has emerged as an area where residents have created a sense of community and worked together to improve the area, despite challenges in living conditions and large differences between those who live there. An activist describes their commitment to Tøyen:

> Tøyen is bigger than those who live here now. People get involved because they have lived here or because they work or have worked here. One person from the sports club still volunteers here even though she has moved. They continue to engage after they have moved.

Those who engage believe that the cause they are engaged in is important, often so important that they continue to help after they have moved and no longer live there. They are happy to contribute for the neighborhood, are enthusiasts preoccupied with inclusion, and do not engage in participation work primarily because they themselves have something to gain from it. Strictly speaking, the value of their apartment could have increased had they advocated for a policy that pushed immigrants out of the area. High social capital is built by people who put a lot of time and energy into building community locally. At the same time, it is interesting to ask how this community arose across quite different groups, from young adults with and without children to immigrant families with many children in social housing, as they do not initially have much in common. One reason could be the importance of meeting places. One backyard, for example, had a hen house that unified people and facilitated encounters between neighbors on a daily basis. Conversations arose and kindergartens came to visit the hen house. People came in contact with others they otherwise would not have talked to.

A reason for the positive development in Tøyen is also the area-based initiative measures that were meant to make the Tøyen area a better place to live. These created an arena for residents where they could interact and influence through organized activities and activity funds. An important measure was free after-school activities. If these had not been free, the children would have returned to their own backyard. There are often large cultural differences between backyards, while in the after-school activities everyone gathers regardless of their background. Another social arena has been the library (Deichman), which probably would not have been as unifying had it not been for the area-based initiatives' efforts. The local school also became a central meeting place for both children and parents across backgrounds. It started with a small group of pioneers of Norwegian parents who chose the local school at Tøyen for their children, even though it was multicultural and there were few other Norwegian children there. Parents' engagement through the Parents Committee has also played a central role in building the community around the school, for example, through the celebration of Norwegian Constitution Day on May 17th, as well as other events. The community around the school and the local football club have helped alleviate some challenges with crime and drugs. Previously, there were a lot of drug addicts in the area. After Sterling, the local football club, was established, the coaches told drug addicts that it is not appropriate to inject drugs where children play. The football club is often out playing in the Tøyen area in the evening.

The community and the area-based initiative have been positive for crime reduction. Families hang out in the park, and drug dealers do not like to be there when their aunt or mother hangs out in the same place, so the park becomes accessible for more people. Districts that do not have the same type of area-based initiatives do not necessarily see the same dynamic. In Gamle Oslo, most believe that residents work together to handle challenges in their local community, and residents feel connected to and help each other. Nearly two-thirds from the survey feel that the residents of the district are interconnected, while in other districts, this percentage is significantly lower. These findings support the media discourse about the Tøyen Village, where residents work together to make it a better place for all who live there. As an employee in the District Gamle Oslo testified:

> The Tøyen Initiative, the Tøyen Campaign, the Tøyen Sports Club, Tøyen Unlimited, a lot of what happens here, the individuals, local boards, Tøyen council and more. We see a fantastic commitment in people here in Tøyen. Many of the people who have lived here for a very long time have had strong visions and dreams to improve the area and make Tøyen better for children and young people. Quite a few new and resourceful people have moved to Tøyen too, and have grown very fond of Tøyen. They engage in the same way. Tøyen school has been the hub. (...) Many say that the Parents Committee at Tøyen school may be the strongest Parents Committee in all of Norway.

Tøyen Unlimited is a community for social entrepreneurs who actively work to build the local community and promote residents' interests against the threat they perceive that gentrification represents—i.e., that rich and resourceful people move into the area and displace current residents as the area becomes more expensive. A social entrepreneur elaborated on how he worked to help locals secure their own income base, specifically to combat the negative consequences of gentrification:

> I have collected data in 15 surveys to gain knowledge about brewing, marketing, barista training, accounting, storytelling, interior design, and customer service. A coffee bar was closed in Tøyen. I found out that the coffee bar owners lacked basic knowledge and have started giving training on this—a coffee bar incubator. The first thing was to find partners. I managed to give free training. I also arranged the Grønland coffee festival in September. It was a great success with participants from Tøyen and

Grønland. We work against gentrification. We are not against what the big chain stores do, but we need the money to circulate in the local community and help the local community.

The social entrepreneur has helped build competence in how to operate a coffee shop to create local jobs, something the big chain stores, which are centrally controlled, do not prioritize. He wants more diverse and locally adapted stores, and his argument for this being a good idea, both socially and economically, is that those who manage to run their own business do not need welfare benefits from the social welfare authorities to survive. His measures are meant to prevent poverty by preserving small businesses and maintaining a multicultural selection of stores. At the same time, he emphasizes that he is not against the big chain stores, but wants to create opportunities for local residents so they are able to compete with the big chains. He wants to be the voice for small companies who are not as good at speaking for themselves. The ambition is to prevent big chain stores from displacing small local shops. The large businesses are well represented and speak well for themselves, while the small ones are vulnerable and need someone who can articulate their needs.

According to informants in the DEMUDIG project, residents' own initiatives often work better than help from public services because the people living in the area understand the local challenges better. For example, the local employment assistance in Tøyen has a 67% success rate because they use youth to guide youth. The local youth feel seen in a different way by them than by the Norwegian Labour and Welfare Administration (NAV), which has less capacity and resources. Giving space for youths' own initiatives makes young people start to take more responsibility and to behave differently.

Local initiatives in Tøyen find they are more effective than the municipal or state organizations because locals have a different insight and commitment. For example, the social entrepreneur Tøyen Unlimited's ambition is to create an arena to help and involve locals in solutions, including those already involved, the entire local community, and other local communities in Norway. They have a local community perspective and use approaches that the NAV cannot use. It is difficult for NAV to work the same way as they must abide by many administrative procedures and have little flexibility.

Engagement in the local community also affects democracy positively. Tøyen Unlimited calls itself a democratization and involvement tool. The solution, according to Tøyen Unlimited, is not for the Oslo municipality to solve all problems through the use of public services. This, they believe, only leads to more exclusion. In their opinion, real co-creation is about giving power back to local communities so they can solve some of their own challenges. Public employees have the best intentions, but are often themselves not aware that the way they implement measures can be challenging and passivating for those who receive the help. What public organizations could have done, they suggest, is let people create their own arena and give them a mandate to fix their own problems. An example of this type of local initiative is youth businesses. At Hersleb high school, a youth business was hired to renovate premises to be used by youth, instead of an architectural firm. Youth know what other young people are interested in and can talk to their friends. A 40-year-old does not speak the same language as 15-year-olds, who may be able to solve the challenge themselves. There are several examples of youth businesses that do everything from sewing clothes, maintaining security, making coffee, giving mental health support, and more. These are initiatives they have taken themselves because they believe they can solve problems in their way. It is a type of approach that can be used to create a more democratic and inclusive city.

The perspective of social entrepreneurs is that public organizations often become too paternalistic and unresponsive in the way they provide help. This leads to less effective help because employees do not understand—and may also not have the prerequisites to understand—those they are supposed to help. The solution outlined by social entrepreneurs is to give more freedom to youth and others in need of assistance to figure out how they can help themselves because they know best what the problem is. It can also be more motivating to take their own initiative rather than being told what to do.

Tøyen Unlimited, which supports local social entrepreneurs, say they see that their measures help the area and that measures they initiate recruit others that also want to contribute. They experience a snowball effect in this way: local residents talk to people they identify with, see people working with ideas, invite friends to these types of activities, and get to know the social entrepreneurs who organize the activities. The measures of the social entrepreneurs are popular and are constantly attracting more participants. They help those who come with their own ideas to put them into practice, but they also help those who lack ideas.

Much of the social capital in the Tøyen area springs from the fact that people have established networks around the school and after-school activities, but the initiatives of social entrepreneurs in Tøyen Unlimited also help. They strengthen youth and people in the area's capacity to address their own challenges and do something about them. This also improves the cohesion and the problem-solving capacities in the area. The DEMUDIG interviews demonstrate how social capital, built up through the efforts of social entrepreneurs, can contribute to making an area more liveable. Those living in the area, or working there as social entrepreneurs, know the area's challenges and have a unique starting point for identifying measures that can be effective in achieving good results.

Sustainable Urban Development

Since sustainable development encompasses several dimensions, it can be unclear, for municipalities and public organizations, what to prioritize. In practice, dilemmas can arise both between and within each of the three sustainability dimensions (Hofstad, 2018a, 2018b). Those who emphasize biodiversity believe that nature has an intrinsic value beyond its utility for humans. In this perspective, the loss of wild animals and ecosystems is a problem in itself. According to the UN's nature panel, biodiversity has never before been as threatened as it is today (IPBES, 2019), and is strained by human agriculture, forestry, and fishing, just to mention some of the challenges. Climate is highlighted as a separate category within environmental sustainability because CO_2 emissions are such a serious and isolated problem that destabilizes the environment and creates challenges for life on Earth, but loss of biodiversity is as threatening to the ecosystem as the climate problem. Many, especially within the environmental movement, are sceptical about whether economic growth is at all compatible with sustainable societal development, arguing that economic growth can be part of the problem. However, the sustainability goals aim for more economic growth, meaning that UN member states see economic growth as part of the solution to create sustainable societies through so-called green growth. Those who see economic growth as part of the problem point out that even green growth usually affects nature negatively, and that growth cannot increase indefinitely. According to this view, it is consumer society and the neoliberal economic system itself that are the cause of our problems. Regardless of these different views on economic growth, there is broad agreement that production must become more sustainable and decrease, at least in the richest countries where consumption is highest.

How Centralization Hinders Local and Sustainable Solutions

Through the Parliamentary Report no. 58 (1996–97) *Miljøvernpolitikk for en bærekraftig utvikling* (Environmental policy for a sustainable development),[1] municipalities are encouraged to facilitate increased participation and also reduce municipalities' environmental impact in the operation of their own organization. This report begins by stating that there is a close connection between global, national, and more local environmental challenges, as environmental challenges are the sum of local actions. Environmental problems often stem from the same types of causes. In the report, all municipalities are encouraged to develop their local *Agenda 21* as an integrated part of municipal planning. However, in Norway, there has been a lack of follow-up on *Agenda 21*. Municipalities have few substantial results to show (Lafferty et al., 2006). In a report from 2001, Future in Our Hands (*Framtiden i våre hender*)[2] concluded that there is a long way to go before any Norwegian local community can be called sustainable. The development is going in the wrong direction, as Norway has increased consumption of most things that burden the environment—to some extent significantly.

As part of environmental policy, public organizations were supposed to show leadership by adapting their procurement strategies to the environment. Public procurers are important customers with a lot of purchasing power and could have accelerated the transition to a more environmentally sustainable society through setting requirements in their tenders. However, the public sector has not been a major driver for sustainability and the environment in procurement. Often, the state's centralization policy also becomes a problem for achieving more circular solutions, including the energy and transport sectors, agriculture, and waste management. Centralized solutions lead to increased traffic, and therefore increased energy consumption. The report generally points to a national policy that promotes consumption growth as a problem (Opoku, 2001).

[1] https://www.regjeringen.no/no/dokumenter/st-meld-nr-58_1996-97/id191317/
[2] https://www.framtiden.no/ Framtiden i våre hender is an idealistic organization advocating for green consumption and resource justice.

There are many institutional barriers to more sustainable procurement. At the same time, not following up on promises for more sustainability can lead to distrust in both local politicians and the administration. People wonder why the plans reported in the local newspapers are not being implemented, and few know who is responsible for the lack of follow-up or for the way the system works. The report states that decisions made centrally and that are sector-oriented are a problem for sustainability (Opoku, 2001). In a later report from the same organization, waste management is reported to be the closest we have come in a circular direction, but what is fundamentally needed are measures that prevent waste from arising, and that preserve and maintain what we already have produced by recycling and reusing it. Only 9% of the world's resources are reused in today's economy, so 91% of the raw materials we extract from nature are not circulated back into the economy and end up as various forms of waste. The solution lies in more comprehensive strategies and broader local influence (Boye, 2019; Dagilienė et al., 2021).

The Future in Our Hands demanded, at the time of their first report in 2001, a cross-sectoral approach to sustainable development. The report highlighted the Eco-lighthouse Initiative as a successful local initiative and pointed to unclear signals and guidelines from the national authorities. According to The Future in Our Hands, the state should have supported initiatives that promote sustainability and reduce consumption growth over 20 years ago, but the opposite has happened. The way the market and the tax system are set up and practiced, and how public organizations purchase goods and services have a significant impact on sustainable transitions in cities. For example, who wins public contracts? Is it smaller sustainable start-ups and local businesses? How easy is it to participate in public tenders for social entrepreneurs and non-profit organizations? The tendency is that public organizations buy more from large companies and less from non-profit organizations (Voldnes, 2012a, 2012b). Requirements in public tenders are hard for smaller companies to live up to, as discussed earlier. For example, obligations to deliver bread to hospitals in the whole country exclude local bakers. Other formal requirements can also exclude smaller suppliers. Large companies can, for example, invest in formal quality systems, often a prerequisite for winning competitions. Nevertheless, buying from only large companies can put public organizations at risk in the longer term if large companies can set the terms for public organizations if there are very few suppliers to choose from. In this way, public organizations can get entangled in a practice that counteracts real competition and that, in the long run, leads to monopolization tendencies and higher prices. The former provide little ground for innovation, and the diversity and quality of products and services can also deteriorate if there is little competition. Smaller companies, on the other hand, are often flexible and innovative, and many can offer sustainable solutions. Public organizations miss out on this if they only buy from large companies (Reichborn-Kjennerud, 2019).

Many public tenders set requirements that make it next to impossible for smaller and often socially sustainable local companies to win contracts. Allowing these companies to deliver to public organizations could nevertheless bring us a step closer to a sustainable economy. Opening up to smaller sustainable initiatives locally could create vibrant local communities that visitors would be interested in visiting. The municipality could, for example, open up unused public buildings to artists and social entrepreneurs, arranging free or affordable events. They could stimulate urban agriculture and local community gardens and see this as part of the municipality's business development, a way to make the place more social and environmentally sustainable, as well as interesting. Today, there are few incentives to create such arenas, the exception being time-limited area-based and project-based initiatives. However, these projects are limited in time, which means that initiatives risk not being continued after the project ends. There are often restrictions preventing funds from being used for wages in certain types of projects, which can lead to buying products and services rather than reusing and repairing (Reichborn-Kjennerud & Svare, 2014).

However, it is easier for public organizations to integrate sustainability considerations into the systems in the way they work today. Within food procurement, one way is to ask large food distributors to include more organic food in their offers. This could solve some challenges, but at the same time, create other problems. For example, in a smaller municipality in eastern Norway, the cook in the after-school activity organization, who used to be able to buy flour from the local organic flour producer, was no longer allowed to buy flour directly from the producer when a new framework agreement was signed. She worked to get organic flour into the range of goods from the new supplier, but found that the flour price increased by 40% when it was included in the assortment of the framework agreement. In the end, the organic flour fell out of range because too few bought it, probably because the price was too high. When the cook then asked for the flour, she was told to instead choose from the types of flour that were available in the digital catalogue. This example shows a disadvantage with central framework agreements. Public organizations do not follow-up well to make sure that they get what they pay for, as it is very time-consuming to follow-up when procurement is centralized.

There has been a centralization and digitization of the procurement function, making local adjustments difficult. It is not considered desirable for employees to spend time finding favorable offers or buying goods and service. Rather, it is seen as more efficient that they choose from the products available in a digital catalogue from the supplier who is delivering on a framework agreement. This organization of procurement can become challenging for smaller places. For example, local stores in small municipalities can lose a large part of their business when the municipality instead chooses to procure through framework agreements. The sale of food represents a large proportion of the local stores' earnings, and when public organizations withdraw their funds to instead buy from large food distributors, local stores can go out of business. This threatens social sustainability in the districts when the local store functions as a local meeting place.[3]

Centralized procurement has made it difficult to buy local food and services, or services from local hotels. Over two decades after The Future in Our Hands report was written, these tendencies are equally strong (Opoku, 2001). There are a number of research and innovation projects trying to explore the possibility of a more sustainable food system from different perspectives (i.e., Fusilli, StrengthToFood, EdiCitNet, Buy sustainably). Many are frustrated that it is difficult to buy locally and fresh. Kindergartens and high schools are often prevented from buying locally and fresh during the season due to exclusive framework agreements that have been entered into centrally. Some kindergartens and schools find this to be practical, but others are frustrated that they cannot buy wholefoods locally. The chefs at the municipality's institutional kitchens can be held accountable if they choose to buy too many local potatoes if this conflicts with exclusive framework agreements that the municipality has entered into.

A reason why public organizations prefer larger food distributors in competitions are logistical challenges. Local purchases are perceived to involve more uncoordinated local traffic, which is considered less environmentally friendly. With framework agreements, the municipalities also get

---

[3] "Kommunen og nærbutikken" (The municipality and the local convenience store), 2022, Distriktssenteret. https://distriktssenteret.no/wp-content/uploads/2020/02/Kommunen-og-narbutikken-1.pdf

a simple setup where all purchases are registered in electronic systems that make it easy to plan and where the invoices are automatically matched against orders and paid. Often, small food producers are not themselves interested in selling directly to the municipality either, because they risk that the large food distributors end their contracts with them, which would make them lose their income. Other challenges are that smaller food producers cannot deliver large enough quantities. They seldom have a varied enough offer and they cannot ensure delivery of products to the municipality throughout the year (Muromskaya, 2022), a requirement municipalities often set to ensure delivery to their institutions, such as nursing homes and kindergartens. Digital marketplaces that enable chefs at institutional kitchens to buy directly from the producers to get more diverse and seasonal products exist,[4] but often, these types of platforms do not satisfy the public organizations' logistical and regulatory needs.

Centralization and regulation can have absurd effects. The Future in Our Hands report gives the example of a local butcher who was allowed to deliver his products to outlets in the same house and adjacent houses with their own kitchen. The problem arose when the goods were to be delivered to an outlet across the road because the store did not meet the requirements for kitchens. To be able to deliver goods to this outlet, the delivery had to go via a central actor. A similar example was given for milk producers in the mountains. Direct delivery between nearby farms and mountain lodges is no longer allowed without the milk first having been sent to the regional dairy. The informants saw this as more expensive and more environmentally damaging than the old arrangements. This centralization policy was linked to health risks for humans and animals, as well as an increased risk of infection (Opoku, 2001). Regulations and procurement systems thus stimulate centralization, while municipalities and public organizations, which are local, are told that they should stimulate a circular economy. More circular systems entail handling their waste more locally and create solutions for local reuse. However, it becomes difficult if the systems prohibit this or make it very unprofitable.

The Future in Our Hands report describes limited freedom to make local purchases when these are not competitive in price. Stavanger municipality went against this practice and made a decision to use local suppliers and producers, allowing for 10% higher prices. It is legal to choose other criteria than price in tenders, but there is still the fear of being sued,

[4] i.e., https://dagens.farm/

coming into the public eye, or getting accused of favoring some suppliers over others. To be able to buy locally requires high legal and contractual knowledge. In smaller places, the municipality may only have a person using 20% of their time on procurement. In these cases, there is simply no time or resources for supplier dialogue or the splitting of contracts to make it easier for smaller suppliers to sell to public organizations. In addition, it is hard for municipalities in a challenging financial situation when local and organic food is often more expensive. However, as of January 1, 2024, there is a new provision in the law that states that climate and environmental concerns should be weighted a minimum of 30% in Norwegian public procurements.

The solution the state agency responsible for procurement policies advises seems simple, namely, to divide the tender into many contracts and dialogue with local providers. However, this requires high competence and a lot of time spent on administrative work that most procurement departments do not have. True sustainability entails giving the opportunity to produce, process, and buy locally, avoid food waste and pesticides, use organic and sustainable methods locally, and buy what is fresh and in season. It also means having control of the sustainability in long supply chains. It is thus a complex picture, where some solutions require more circular, local, and organic production and consumption. A more sustainable organization of the food system could also represent an opportunity for creating inclusive local jobs, but the Norwegian grocery market is concentrated around a few grocery chains, with high entry barriers. The prices are higher and the selection poorer than in other European countries, and competition is limited.[5] This chapter has pointed out some hindrances for sustainable local transitions. When decisions are centralized, it becomes more difficult to focus on local sustainable solutions.

REFERENCES

Agger, A., & Jensen, J. O. (2015). Area-based initiatives—And their work in bonding, bridging and linking social capital. *European Planning Studies, 23*(10), 2045–2061.

---

[5] Konkurransetilsynets dagligvare rapport 2022. Konkurransetilsynet, Bergen kommune. https://konkurransetilsynet.no/wp-content/uploads/2022/12/Konkurransetilsynets-dagligvarerapport-2022.pdf

Barthes, R. (1991). *Mytologier—Om mytene i den moderne tids hverdag.* Gyldendal norsk forlag.
Bourdieu, P. (1995). *Distinksjonen—En sosiologisk kritikk av dømmekraften.* Pax Forlag A/S.
Boye, E. (2019). Sirkulær framtid–om skiftet fra lineær til sirkulær økonomi. *Framtiden i våre hender.* Rapport August 2019, 5–59.
Dagilienė, L., Varaniūtė, V., & Bruneckienė, J. (2021). Local governments' perspective on implementing the circular economy: A framework for future solutions. *Journal of Cleaner Production, 310,* 127340.
Dinnie, K. (2011). *City branding: Theory and cases.* Palgrave Macmillan.
Falkum, E., Nordrik, B., Wathne, C. T., Drange, I., Hansen, P. B., Dahl, E. M., Kuldova, T., & Underthun, A. (2022). *Måling og styring av arbeidstid–Medbestemmelsesbarometeret 2021.* AFI-rapport 2022, 01.
Florida, R. L. (2012). *The rise of the creative class: Revisited.* Basic Books.
Granovetter, M. S. (1973). The strength of weak ties. *American Journal of Sociology, 78*(6), 1360–1380.
Hanssen, G. S. (2021). Medvirkningens idélandskap i Dahlgren, K., Linderud, T. & Schreiner, K. (red) *Forankring fryder: En bok om medvirkning i byutvikling og arkitektur* (pp. 50–65). Universitetsforlaget.
Hanssen, G. S., & Aarsæther, N. (Eds.). (2018). *Plan-og bygningsloven 2008: En lov for vår tid?.* Universitetsforlaget.
Hanssen, G. S., Hofstad, H., & Saglie, I. L. (Eds.). (2015). *Kompakt byutvikling. Muligheter og utfordringer.* Universitetsforlaget.
Hermansen, T. (2013). Ble det en bedre stat? *Stat & Styring, 23*(2), 24–25. https://doi.org/10.18261/ISSN0809-750X-2013-02-10
Hofstad, H. (2018a). Bærekraftig planlegging for framtida? In G. S. Hanssen & N. Aarsæther (Eds.), *Pbl (2008)–en lov for vår tid?* (pp. 203–221). Universitetsforlaget.
Hofstad, H. (2018b). Folkehelse—proaktivt grep i pbl.2008, hva er status ti år etter? In G. S. Hanssen, & N. Aarsæther (Eds.), *Pbl (2008)–en lov for vår tid?* Universitetsforlaget.
Hovik, S., Giannoumis, G. A., Reichborn-Kjennerud, K., Ruano, J. M., McShane, I., & Legard, S. (2022). *Citizen Participation in the information society: Comparing participatory channels in urban development.* Springer Nature.
Innset, O. (2020). *Markedsvendingen: Nyliberalismens historie i Norge.* Fagbokforlaget.
IPBES. (2019). Global assessment report of the Intergovernmental Science-Policy Platform on Biodiversity and Ecosystem Services. In E. S. Brondízio, J. Settele, S. Díaz, & H. T. Ngo (Eds.), *IPBES Secretariat.*
Lafferty, W., Aall, C., Lindseth, G., & Norland, I. T. (2006). *Lokal Agenda 21 I Norge: Så mye hadde vi–så mye ga vi bort–så mye har vi igjen.* Unipub.

Legard, S., McShane, I., & Ruano, J. M. (2022). What explains the degree of e-participation? A comparison of the adoption of digital participation platforms in Oslo, Melbourne and Madrid. *Information Polity, 28*(3), 359–375.

Linstad, A. (2018). Kraftig kritikk av Tøyenløftet i ny rapport. 'De stille stemmene' ble ikke hørt. *Vårt Oslo*, 17, September 2018. https://www.vartoslo.no/arnsten-linstad-gamle-oslo-hanna-marcussen/kraftig-kritikk-av-toyenloftet-i-ny-rapport-de-stille-stemmene-ble-ikke-hort/182357

Muromskaya, M. (2022). Hvorfor klarer ikke kommunene å kjøpe inn lokal og bærekraftig mat? *Forskning.no*, 17, October 2022.

Opoku, H. (2001). Lokal handling—nasjonal famling. Når nasjonal politikk hindrer lokalt miljøarbeid. Framtiden i våre henders forskningsinstitutt. Rapport May 2001.

Pistor, K. (2019). *The code of capital: How the law creates wealth and inequality*. Princeton University Press.

Pløger, J. (2002). *Kommunikativ planlegging og demokrati*. Norsk institutt for by-og regionforskning.

Putnam, R. D. (1993). *Making democracy work: Civic traditions in modern Italy*. Princeton University Press.

Putnam, R. D. (2015). Bowling alone: America's declining social capital. In *The city reader* (pp. 188–196). Routledge.

Reichborn-Kjennerud, K. (1997). *Gata er mitt galleri: en analyse av estetiske og sosiale aspekter ved graffitisubkulturen i Oslo* (Master's thesis), University of Oslo.

Reichborn-Kjennerud, K. (2019). Konkurranseutsettingen ødelegger konkurransen, Aftenposten, 5 December 2019. https://www.aftenposten.no/meninger/debatt/i/kJPV9j/konkurranseutsettingen-oedelegger-konkurransen-reichborn-kjennerud

Reichborn-Kjennerud, K., McShane, I., Middha, B., & Ruano, J. M. (2021). Exploring the relationship between trust and participatory processes: Participation in urban development in Oslo, Madrid and Melbourne. *Nordic Journal of Urban Studies, 1*(2), 94–112.

Reichborn-Kjennerud, K., & Ophaug, E. (2018). Resident participation in an era of societal self-organisation: The Public administrative response in Tøyen. *Scandinavian Journal of Public Administration, 22*(2), 65–87.

Reichborn-Kjennerud, K., & Svare, H. (2014). Entrepreneurial growth strategies: The female touch. *International Journal of Gender and Entrepreneurship, 6*(2), 181–199. https://doi.org/10.1108/IJGE-04-2013-0043

Sachs Olsen, C. (2021) *Fremtidsfabrikken. Fra bevaringsscenarioer til transformative scenarioer i planprosesser* i "Improvisasjon. Byliv mellom plan og planløshet". Spartacus Forlag AS / Scandinavian Academic Press. Kristiansand, 131–150.

Sintomer, Y., Herzberg, C., & Röcke, A. (2008). Participatory budgeting in Europe: Potentials and challenges. *International Journal of Urban and Regional Research, 32*(1), 164–178.

Voldnes, F. (2012a). Folkevalgt styring eller markedsstyring? *Samfunn og økonomi, 2*, 6–27.

Voldnes, F. (2012b). *Markedsretting av offentlig sektor: Virkemidler og alternativer.* Fagforbundet. https://assets-global.website-files.com/65e884f8fffb6d61 0d77c46d/65fc3739f69e601b3352005b_Markedsretting%20des%20 2012.pdf

Zukin, S. (2012). Whose culture? Whose city? In J. Lin & C. Mele (Eds.), *The urban sociology reader* (pp. 363–371). Routledge.

CHAPTER 7

How to Create Socially Sustainable Places

Abstract In our efforts for more sustainable systems, we often adjust the current situation instead of finding new solutions. These preservation scenarios have little room for the type of radical societal change that today's increasing social and environmental challenges demand, but there are always alternatives. This chapter plays with different ways of thinking, understanding, organizing, collaborating, and prioritizing in cities that could potentially take us towards more sustainable and inclusive societies. We need more flexible systems that allow place-based solutions to develop more organically, and municipalities should have departments responsible for interdisciplinary local community work. Physical meeting places are important to allow more social and spontaneous city life, and it is important to ensure that local communities get to participate in urban development to safeguard liveability. Public health, and environmental and social sustainability often go hand-in-hand.

Keywords Community Plan • Public health • Area-based initiative • Planning • Urban governance

It is easier to identify problems than to solve them, but how can we solve urban development in a better way? What alternatives exist? Much indicates that New Public Management (NPM) has increased the fragmentation of public organizations and made it harder for them to see complex social problems holistically. This makes sustainable solutions harder to identify. As seen, the way Management by Objectives and Results (MBOR) is implemented can challenge co-creation and sustainability, which are new ideals in municipal community planning. The community plan of municipalities is intended to be a management tool, ideally a vision, a kind of future dream image of the municipality that helps us get there. The vision should be operationalized, broken down into goals and action plans, viewed across sectors, and divided into themes, goals, and results. The latter should be measurable within one- and four-year periods when the action and community plans are to be renewed. It seems sensible to point out the direction for a municipality by formulating overarching goals, breaking them down into concrete sub-goals, and then specifying what measures need be taken for these goals and sub-goals to be achieved. However, the question is how the systems work in practice. As already seen, the way decisions are implemented does not always create the results decision-makers intended. In reality, much power lies in the actual implementation of the decisions. The organization and management of systems in the public sector have a decisive impact on the result, on who gets influence over and benefits from the measures.

The Norwegian *Planning and Building Act* of 2008 also incorporates public health as a purpose for planning, thus aligning with the *Norwegian Public Health Act* of 2011. The purpose is:

> to contribute to societal development that promotes public health and reduces social inequalities in health. Public health work shall promote the population's health, well-being and good social and environmental conditions, and contribute to the prevention of mental and somatic illnesses, disorders or injuries.[1]

The emphasis is on general, universal, and preventive measures. Public health work is focused equally as much on promoting health and well-being as on preventing ill health and identifying factors that affect health positively or negatively. Factors influencing health are found in many

---

[1] *The Norwegian Public Health Act.* https://www.regjeringen.no/globalassets/upload/hod/hoeringer-fha_fos/123.pdf

sectors of society and in different arenas, such as within education and the workplace. Therefore, in public health work, measures are implemented primarily outside of the health service, where people live, work, and go to school. People's health is, in other words, closely linked to how we organize and structure society.

Municipalities must set public health as a goal, prioritize it in planning, and make it operational and possible to implement using diverse tools (Hofstad, 2018a, 2018b). The *Planning and Building Act* of 2008 in itself does not seem to represent the biggest problem for a more sustainable development in urban development, and the law emphasizes both public health and social sustainability. It is more the interpretation and the practical operationalization that appear to be the problem. Planners seem to embrace the most business-friendly aspects of the law, such as the aforementioned densification policy, without simultaneously emphasizing social sustainability to the extent required. Social sustainability becomes especially important as densification policy creates a greater need to secure community arenas (Hanssen 2021).

As already seen, when development becomes too focused on business actors' interests, residents often get little influence over development in their area, despite participation being politically desired as a measure to improve local democracy (Ruano and Reichborn-Kjennerud 2021). The municipality enters into contracts with large developers before residents are invited to express their opinion, and little consideration is given to the qualities of the area as a whole while building more and more densely. The main focus on efficiency and profit thus has negative implications for the local environment and democracy in urban development. Possible solutions to this are discussed below.

The User, the Resident, and the Place Must be at the Centre

Some politicians are responsible for culture, some for upbringing, and others for planning. The silo division in administration is also reflected at the political level. Even though it is sensible to specialize and distribute tasks, this creates challenges in cases where it is best to view problems across sectors. Leaders and employees become excessively concerned with what is their area of responsibility and have little room for manoeuvre to take other considerations into account. When measures benefit another organization, there are no incentives to consider concerns other than the organization's own Key Performance Indicators (KPI) and budget. This type of focus can create worse results than what is optimal. If you build a city that caters to cars and it is dangerous to cycle, then people are less likely to cycle to work. This results in people moving their bodies less in their daily lives, and could lead to lifestyle diseases that could put pressure on the health budget in the long run. If we build a city without accessible low threshold meeting places for different groups, it could contribute to vulnerable children and young people seeking arenas that give them unhealthy impulses. Elderly persons could become more passive and lonelier and thus, in need of more help from the public health service. Trying to solve complex challenges in simple ways is not necessarily a good idea in the long run.

Much can be said about how existing systems work. Some things work well, but there are always things that can be improved, even in the most well-organized municipality. Budgets also set some boundaries, as municipalities do not have unlimited resources and most have to prioritize solving statutory services, such as child welfare and home care services. A lot is to be achieved with scarce public funds. Employees may also need to shield themselves from unrealistic expectations from citizens. They can do this by sticking to the requirements and responsibilities that have been formally assigned to them.

In the EdiCitNet project,[2] municipal employees shared how they feel that there is little financial room to prioritize local community work, which they believe could contribute to several different good purposes simultaneously, such as preventing dementia and crime, and creating open local meeting places for people to meet and socialize. At the same time, it is more tangible for politicians to allocate money to activities that can be counted, rather than investing in arenas like public libraries, parks, and local meeting places. The results of policies are far too often understood as the number of counted units according to predetermined parameters and targets. Local community work and areas open to the community, when operated in the right way, can create value over time, but they may not be immediately visible, and thus, possible to count.

The population in Norway and many Western countries is aging. People need more help as they age, so it is understandable that the authorities are

---

[2] See annex 1.

trying to squeeze the most out of every penny. At the same time, taking a preventative approach can be a more effective strategy in the long run. Building infrastructure and arenas so that individuals and networks in local communities can help themselves and each other through collective solutions could address several issues simultaneously. For example, if municipalities were to have overarching departments or units responsible for local community work and public health, the municipality could potentially work differently and more interdisciplinary to create long-term good results, prevent dropout from school and work, prevent crime, loneliness, and lifestyle diseases, and improve physical and mental health—areas that cost society a lot both socially and economically.

The way local community initiatives survive today is by demonstrating how they are relevant for public organizations' objectives and may contribute positively to different budgets (Izquierdo and Curtis 2022; Plassnig et al. 2022). This can be limiting for their contributions. Maybe it could be an advantage with a more flexible system that allows place-based solutions to develop more organically instead. As a participant with a coordinating role in the EdiCitNet[3] project explained:

> I work with many projects where we create places. We gather the actors who want to cooperate. We don't know what the goal is or what the result will be, initially. You might end up somewhere completely different from where you started. (...) It's a lot about relationships. If you have good relationships, you can achieve a lot. If everyone follows a written bureaucratic plan, then nothing happens.

The project mentioned in the quote is a local community initiative that developed into a community garden, test beds, art projects, meeting places, restoration, and organic cultivation, which in turn, led to all kinds of collaborations with the local school, kindergartens, and the shopping centre in the area. The coordinator said the following about their working method:

> If we can connect with people, we can achieve anything. If you are told what to do, then you do it, but magic is not created. You need to have safe relationships. What do you have to build on if you do not have those relationships? What do you have then?

---

[3] See annex 1.

The value these initiatives contribute can be linked to better well-being. Those who visit the local community garden may finally get out of the house and talk to someone. People could receive positive encouragement, learn something new, and experience more joy, which can help tackle challenges like feelings of isolation and loneliness. Results like these are difficult to measure. However, the question is whether measurement is the most important thing. What is important is that public organizations ensure that local communities remain open and inclusive for all groups, so that people can come and know they are welcome. The public responsibility should be to help avoid open or hidden barriers to use the place. If these measures work well, this will show in statistics in the long run.

In the EdiCitNet[4] project, we observed that the financing of local community gardens, social entrepreneurs, and social initiatives is fragmented and unpredictable. Both state and municipal grant schemes are difficult to get an overview of, and few funds cover expenses for operations. In Oslo municipality, there are several funds relevant for urban agriculture, but little coordination. What you can apply for depends on which district you live in. Usually, projects receive support for investment and not the work people put in, making it cheaper to buy soil and equipment rather than composting or repairing, which would make it more sustainable.

When we are market-driven, responsibility for the community and its meeting places becomes fragmented. Also, ensuring meeting places through project grants can be challenging, as these are low, time limited, and unpredictable. You need a specific competence to understand how to write proposals and apply correctly. Each public organization that contributes with money requires a certain amount of self-financing, and beneficiaries must report on the objectives of and the results to each funder. In the EdiCitNet project, we observed how the green and social entrepreneurs wore themselves out on proposal writing to get budgets to balance with demands for self-financing. Some went bankrupt.

Through the EdiCitNet project, we learned about Trosterudparken, an area in the suburbs of Oslo. The park is part of an area-based initiative in Groruddalen, in the northeast of the city. The area-based initiative has accomplished good results through an interdisciplinary work method. Centrally located in the park's area is a small manor that was previously a psychiatric hospital run by Dr. Dedichen. The area has beautiful old buildings, but also many grey asphalt areas, some old greenhouses, and a barn.

---

[4] See annex 1 and https://www.edicitnet.com/

The buildings have been poorly maintained and people have been scared to go there. They believed that the small manor was a private residence and therefore not accessible. The road, trees, and buildings on the site are owned by five different municipal agencies, making it difficult for the municipality to achieve anything in the park. The area-based initiative started their work with Trosterudparken, based on an initiative from the local community. They proposed a plan for Trosterud, inspired by Dr. Dedichen. In his time, he was interested in cultivation and art, so these have become an important inspiration for the park, where they try to create a link between the circular economy and urban agriculture, calling themselves the circular village of Trosterud. The project manager for the initiative in Trosterudparken works differently than municipal agencies. She did not start by building benches. The residents contacted her, the project manager asked if they needed benches, and then they brought old benches, refurbished them, and put them out for free. The municipality was responsive to the local community, what they wanted, and had been working on. They did not want a newly refurbished recycling station, but a place where they could repair things themselves. They wanted to do it locally, and get a little dirty while doing it. This type of approach to citizen involvement seems to work. It takes a lot of time, but when the meeting places are finished, there are also people who use them. It takes time to get to know each other and find solutions together, as different people want to contribute with different things. Some want to cultivate, while others want to refurbish benches. The key lies in multi-use: the place should be multifunctional and possible to use for everyone. In this case, the solution became a circular meeting place with workshops, benches and tables, cultivation, employment, a recycling station, furniture, and repair.

The initiative in Trosterudparken plans to involve and pay people in the local community for working there and to require that the contractors bring along young people to do simple tasks. All of this is supposed to bring more life to Trosterudparken, which was previously perceived as dark and scary. The project manager spoke to the Norwegian Labour and Welfare Administration (NAV), schools, and kindergartens and asked: What do young people who do not complete high school need? The plan is to have vocational teachers in various positions so youth can acquire formal competence with time. Nature, culture, neighborhood, and reuse are connected through activities in the park. The project creates an annual wheel with activities that will take place at the same time each year, and the objective is for neighborhood residents to adopt the plan. The project has come a long way, but much remains to be done. When the area-based initiative ends, the area will again be managed through the municipality's regular agencies, which is seen as a risk, as expressed by the project manager:

> There is a lot of new municipal theory, but not much happens in practice when it comes to urban agriculture and reuse.

The local community supports the Trosterud initiative. The unit for volunteering and meeting places in the area also helps out, but for Trosterudparken to become the meeting place the local community wants even after the area-based initiative ends, negotiations must be conducted and agreements on rents agreed on so that the initiative can continue to live on. Shared use agreements may be a solution to cover the costs.

Oslo municipality is strongly committed to the green shift. It has strategies for urban agriculture and wants more mini recycling stations in the city, so opportunities are there. Still, it would be an advantage to have more bottom-up initiatives. The systemic problem must also be addressed. There are many employees who want to improve the way things work, but they have a narrow area of responsibility and a diminishing and narrow scope of authority. The system itself makes it difficult to take holistic responsibility, and it becomes too complex for individual employees to change the system from within.

Sustainability cannot be interpreted as good scores on individual KPI. That is a compliance-oriented approach that does not address systemic challenges (Kuldova 2022). Silo organization makes sustainable development difficult. The original idea in NPM was that standardization and result units would make it easier to compare goal achievement across organizations, but measuring in result units does not improve interaction and cooperation across these units. The idea in market management is that best practice in one organization should uplift and inspire other organizations to work better. Some procedures may be time-saving and appropriate to standardize, but very often it is smarter not to standardize, as it is frequently wiser to cultivate the uniqueness of the place, which can raise the attractiveness of an area for its own residents, future residents, and visitors to the municipality (Reichborn-Kjennerud and Svare 2014). This type of development could be an alternative to the global consumer society, which tends towards similar products and similar thoughts, without local character, both aesthetically and in terms of activities and lifestyles.

The Uniqueness of a Place Can Be its Gold

The state encourages municipalities to be innovative through various innovation support schemes. However, these are, in most cases, set up to stimulate the next large growth company that can become a cornerstone for the local community and economic locomotive for the municipality. Innovation funders hardly focus on the fact that stimulating the uniqueness of places, getting small and interesting niche initiatives to flourish, can be innovation (Reichborn-Kjennerud and Svare 2014). Instead, high tech and large growth companies are often equated with innovative solutions. Few believe that social innovation and sustainability can go hand-in-hand in shaping interesting places that create good living conditions for residents and increase the place's attractiveness (Reichborn-Kjennerud and Svare 2014).

Many phenomena we see in cities today are present in peripheral areas as well, aided by digitalization. Distinctions that still remain between larger and smaller places are the variation of offers available, density, and the number of people living in the same place. People interact differently in more densely populated areas. Density and large, varied populations reduce familiarity and common frames of reference. These phenomena have been described by the classics of sociology: Simmel, Goffman, and Tönnies. When residents no longer know each other personally, there is less social control. Safety and security must then be ensured in more formalized ways. The positive thing about more formal ways and less social control is that anonymity can offer more freedom and new ways of interacting with people, but anonymity can also lead to more loneliness and a diminished feeling of belonging. However, village-like solidarity can perhaps be formed under the right conditions in cities as well. Several researchers claim this to be the case. There are examples of villages in cities, including the local community built up in Tøyen close to Oslo city centre. City-like arenas can also be created in smaller places, and the municipality can stimulate local meeting places. This is something different and more than building physical places and locations. Although physical meeting places are an important starting point for social and spontaneous city life, they are not sufficient (Tjora 2018). However, the question is what responsibility municipalities and public organizations feel they have to stimulate this social city life and how they can do it.

Closing down libraries and raising prices for the use of public swimming pools makes sense from a neoliberal perspective. Maintenance may be needed for the latter. Perhaps the KPIs show that young people read fewer books and that the libraries therefore did not reach their objectives. This then quickly becomes an argument for closing down these arenas, these commons. What is perceived as useful for society and for a library could, for example, be the number of books lent out. While an alternative way to see benefit is to consider that these meeting places can create good impulses for both younger and older residents, and who can meet people there and gain access to resources that push them in the right direction in life. It is not easy to measure, but it can be good for public health. It can appear disproportionately expensive, in a short-term perspective, to keep these arenas if the result that is counted is the number of books lent out.

CHALLENGES OF CREATING UNIQUE AND ATTRACTIVE PLACES

When gentrification occurs and wealthier residents and businesses are attracted to an area, the uniqueness, which initially made a place interesting, is often lost. Gentrification is a process where a run-down area with challenging living conditions—and a more mixed population with gradual physical upgrades—becomes prosperous and well-maintained. Towards the end of the gentrification process, the area appears commercial because the only businesses that can afford to rent are chain stores and only the wealthy can afford to buy apartments in the area (Reichborn-Kjennerud et al. 2021). Wealthy businesses and chain stores take over and displace the small unique shops that can no longer afford to pay the rent. The gentrification process is largely market-driven, but state and municipal maintenance and investments are also drivers. An area becomes popular and prices increase because of state investments, private upgrades, and artists moving in, and interesting things start to happen culturally. Often, the gentrification process starts as a combination of these three phenomena (Lees et al. 2016).

Many municipalities have been inspired by Bilbao, in northern Spain, which was previously a poor industrial city and is now a known cultural destination. We can see the same phenomenon in a number of Norwegian cities, including Kristiansand, which has transformed the grain silo by the seafront into a modern museum. Many cities have succeeded with these strategies and attract tourists. This creates challenges in turn. For cities like Madrid and Barcelona, their popularity has led to very high housing prices. More use of Airbnb also drives living costs up (Reichborn-Kjennerud et al. 2021). The city becomes an entertainment machine for tourists, while the local population with more moderate and lower wages, and smaller businesses are displaced because the city becomes too expensive to live in. This type of tourism can lead to problems for both nature and the local population, and is not necessarily sustainable. Another example is Venice and the cruise boats that burden the infrastructure and pollute the city. In Norway, an example could be the Norwegian mountain range, where tourists, at certain popular destinations, disturb wildlife and destroy nature.

In central residential areas, residents often have diverse backgrounds and different interests. Thus, community building and working together for the area's interests become more challenging. One of our informants from a neighborhood organization explained:

> The Fuencarral-El Pardo district is the largest in Madrid and is very heterogeneous, with many neighborhoods that are different from each other and large income differences. Therefore, it is sometimes difficult to speak on behalf of the district, even though we have methods to coordinate the different neighborhood movements.

Another challenge, especially for Madrid, but to some extent also for Oslo and Melbourne, is the trade-off between the interests of tourists and those who live in the area, especially when it comes to Airbnb. As explained by an informant from a neighborhood association:

> The most important thing in a neighborhood is that the municipal regulations are followed, that the bars close when they should, that people don't drink in the street. That apartments are not rented out to tourists without it being regulated. In a neighborhood, consideration must be given to those who live there, not just to the visitors.

At the same time, the sense of community varies in different neighborhoods, and is important for an effective defence of the neighborhood's interests. In a study of four districts in Barcelona and New York City, the authors compare neighborhoods with varying degrees of social capital (Parés et al. 2017). The book analyses neighborhood resilience and describes community engagement as a prerequisite for social capital. Community engagement is needed to get people to work for the community at the neighborhood level, and social capital makes up the community engagement necessary to defend the neighborhood's community values. It requires the ability to negotiate, cooperate, interact, and exchange experiences (Parés et al. 2017).

How to Move in a More Sustainable Direction

How can we move more towards sustainability in practical planning? In urban development and planning processes, scenarios are often used as tools in planning. Unfortunately, scenarios usually project current trends and tendencies into the future. Instead of promoting radical alternatives to today's systems, scenarios preserve the existing ones (Sachs Olsen 2021). Scenarios based on today's structures leave little room for debate around other alternatives, and we end up adjusting the situation according to existing social structures. These conservation scenarios have little room for the type of radical social change needed to handle the social and environmental challenges we face as humans. The Covid-19 pandemic, polarization, populism, and global warming clearly show that the prevailing economic system cannot continue. There is a need to design radically different social structures that better safeguard social justice and sustainability (Boye 2019).

The city is a social construction with potential for change, not only a physically definable geographical unit. The city is created, but in planning, the city is seen from a large-scale perspective based on rational principles. The lived political and social life and the imaginary, suppressed, and irrational dimensions of society, which take place on a microscale, are not taken into account. Often, planning tools and illustrations exclude lived life, and do not incorporate the processes that are constantly changing (Sachs Olsen 2021).

City governance has historically been top-down, and is there to control the city. It is seen as a structure rather than a social and embodied process in constant change. This type of ordering structure is imposed and helps create the city. Even though these organizing structures are introduced with the best intentions, they do not always function well. Positivist approaches in planning, where the planners are seen as neutral technocrats, have been criticized. However, the neoliberal form of planning, which in principle means governance through commercial forces' interests, also takes few human and environmental considerations. If the previous planning perspective omitted the dynamics and energy of the city, the neoliberal planning practice does something similar by placing too one-sided an emphasis on profit, which can come at the expense of human needs (Sachs Olsen 2021).

In recent decades, this rational and top-down approach has been challenged by, among others, urban planner Patsy Healey (2006), who launched a communicative turn in planning. Proponents of this approach want a more inclusive planning that takes into account power inequality and conflicting interests, social relations, and cultural diversity. Healey pointed out that the planner's most important role is to explore who has an interest in a matter. This is done through an analysis that identifies who the stakeholders are. Then, the planners base their work on the individuals' and organizations' particular interests. In practice, however, planners overlook the active role they themselves, developers, and architects play in defining who holds which interests. Who gets and can get involved is always limited. These processes can be seen as part of an ever-increasing depoliticization of society where the political is weakened in favor of a consensus-based and technocratic form of participation and governance. Major societal issues are handled in such processes. The political is thus reduced to a question of administrative governance, which ignores inherent societal contradictions and conflicts, and the solutions that come out of these processes are presented as the only possible alternatives. The urban development debate is characterized by this rhetoric and leads to a lack of willingness and ability to explore and imagine radical change in the planning and governance of cities (Sachs Ohlsen 2021).

It is difficult to create an open process in planning, perhaps because important material and symbolic resources are at stake. Consultations often lead to different actors presenting clear, strong, and distinct views from fear of missing out on their interests, making it difficult to experiment with more open positions and visions because everyone is looking after their own interests. Therefore, planning must take place in a context where interests are not at stake. This could be a planning workshop where planners and local actors collectively develop an idea or concept for urban and place development. This type of setting can be unofficial and is often only advisory. It is easier to experiment with alternatives to traditional plans and solutions without having to risk social and political consequences, and utopian thinking is important for creating opportunities for radical change. This approach creates a greater openness for imagination and dreams alongside the sober analysis of urban researchers and planners (Sachs Olsen 2021).

Planning usually takes place centrally in a municipality, but processes that influence living conditions and lived life locally also take place outside the planning departments. Planning could therefore include the district level and communities more. The districts in larger Norwegian cities have little power in urban planning. However, through area-based initiatives in deprived areas, some districts have been given authority and resources to make improvements in their area. However, even with area-based initiatives, it is not a given that the residents feel that they are getting their needs met. The area-based initiative in one of Oslo's central districts, Tøyen, is an example of this (Reichborn-Kjennerud et al. 2021).

In this chapter, the question whether there exist any alternatives to today's urban governance was asked. Can we have other visions for how we want to live? Can we solve urban development in a better way? Some alternatives have been highlighted, involving bringing back nature and the social, and creating villages in the city. Facilitating open and free areas for residents and prioritizing the commons more are other suggestions. This is even more important now with the current densification policy. An idea could be to organize overarching departments and divisions responsible for the local community, community development, and public health. Ensuring that local communities get to participate in determining urban development in their area could also contribute to securing better living conditions, as well as putting the residents at the centre by collaborating across departments and ministries. This represents some possible directions for a more sustainable urban development.

References

Boye, E. (2019). Sirkulær framtid–om skiftet fra lineær til sirkulær økonomi. *Framtiden i våre hender*. Rapport August 2019, 5–59.

Hanssen, G. S. (2021). Medvirkningens idélandskap i Dahlgren, K., Linderud, T. & Schreiner, K. (red) *Forankring fryder: En bok om medvirkning i byutvikling og arkitektur* (pp. 50–65), Universitetsforlaget.

Healey, P. (2006). *Urban complexity and spatial strategies: Towards a relational planning for our times*. Routledge.

Hofstad, H. (2018a). Bærekraftig planlegging for framtida? In G. S. Hanssen & N. Aarsæther (Eds.), *Pbl (2008)–en lov for vår tid?* (pp. 203–221). Universitetsforlaget.

Hofstad, H. (2018b). Folkehelse—proaktivt grep i pbl.2008, hva er status ti år etter? In G. S. Hanssen & N. Aarsæther (Eds.), *Pbl (2008)–en lov for vår tid?* (pp. 223–240). Universitetsforlaget.

Izquierdo, L. M., & Curtis, A. (2022). *Diamond model: Userguide*. EdiCitNet. https://www.edicitnet.com/wp-content/uploads/Diamond-Model-User-Guide.pdf

Kuldova, T. Ø. (2022). *Compliance-industrial complex: The operating system of a pre-crime society*. Palgrave Pivot. https://doi.org/10.1007/978-3-031-19224-1

Lees, L., Shin, H. B., & López-Morales, E. (2016). *Planetary gentrification*. John Wiley & Sons.

Parés, M., Ospina, S. M., & Subirats, J. (Eds.). (2017). *Social innovation and democratic leadership: Communities and social change from below*. Edward Elgar Publishing.

Plassnig, S. N., Pettit, M., Reichborn-Kjennerud, K., & Säumel, I. (2022). Successful scaling of Edible City Solutions to promote food citizenship and sustainability in food system transitions. *Frontiers in Sustainable Cities, 4*, 190.

Reichborn-Kjennerud, K., de la Fuente, J. R., & Sorando, D. (2021). Ways to gain influence for residents in two gentrifying neighborhoods: A comparison between Tøyen in Oslo and Lavapiés in Madrid. *Papeles de Población, 27*(110), 109–137. https://rppoblacion.uaemex.mx/article/view/16158

Reichborn-Kjennerud, K., & Svare, H. (2014). Entrepreneurial growth strategies: The female touch. *International Journal of Gender and Entrepreneurship, 6*(2), 181–199. https://doi.org/10.1108/IJGE-04-2013-0043

Ruano, J. M., & Reichborn-Kjennerud, K. (2022). Inside the black box: Perspectives and attitudes of civil servants on citizen participation. In S. Hovik, A. Giannoumis, K. Reichborn-Kjennerud, J. M. Ruano, I. McShane, & S. Legard (Eds.), *Citizen participation in the information society* (pp. 71–95). Palgrave Macmillan.

Sachs Olsen, C. (2021) *Fremtidsfabrikken. Fra bevaringsscenarioer til transformative scenarioer i planprosesse*r i "Improvisasjon. Byliv mellom plan og planløshet". Spartacus Forlag AS / Scandinavian Academic Press. Kristiansand, 131–150.

Tjora, A. (2018). *Hva er fellesskap*. Universitetsforlaget.

CHAPTER 8

Solutions for the Future

Abstract The human species collectively faces a potential breakdown of the Earth's ecological capacity. This last chapter suggests that we must change our values, mindset, and thinking to go in a more sustainable direction. The Earth Charter can represent this type of needed alternative way of thinking. It encompasses a spiritual intelligence also embedded in the philosophy of deep ecology. To avoid a development threatening the Earth's ecological capacity, the state and municipalities must organize themselves differently in coming years. This may involve greater focus on the commons and involving residents more in organizing themselves, sharing common goods, and building good local communities. Future public institutions may perhaps play on this dynamic of trust, which we now see a desire for through demands for a trust reform in Norway.

Keywords Earth Charter • Circular systems • Post-neoliberal society • Spiritual intelligence • Collective action • Common goods

To avoid economic collapse and a development threatening the Earth's ecological capacity, the state and municipalities must organize themselves differently in coming years. Public organizations must go in a more sustainable direction that is also beneficial for public health. This must involve greater focus on the commons, where residents are involved in organizing themselves.

Excessive competition and individualization have come at the expense of cooperation. A one-sided focus on production and control is not good for well-being. Far too many experience this reality as living in a machine. Democracy, the social, and the collective are values still seen as fundamental by many people, but these values are undermined on a daily basis by our management and governance systems. That politicians govern through market regulation is not a problem isolated to urban planning and development, but permeates all policy areas. The use of Management by Objectives and Results (MBOR) and the increased use of the market and management through contracts includes all sectors. With New Public Management (NPM), the plan was to get more out of existing resources while simultaneously improving quality through efficiency and standardization. It is an enticing but not new idea, having reappeared at regular intervals throughout history (Velten, 2022). Election promises, demands, and expectations from citizens drive this tendency, which negatively affects our lives. We experience more pressure, mistrust, and control—as workers, users and even customers, residents in local communities, and citizens—while there is less room for the commons, which is key for people's health and well-being. In this so-called efficient system, the population is raised to become useful and efficient consumers who do not question the system and the way it works (Innset, 2020). This way of organizing society does not yield good social and environmental sustainability effects. Modern education systems contribute to shaping these neoliberal subjects, who are taught to see their activities as investments for the maximum value for money. Increasingly, people, in addition to being workers, are not only consumers but also investors who support the current economic system in competition with their fellow human beings. They are decreasingly reflexive citizens of a democracy where decisions are made politically. Instead, we have neoliberal subjects subjectivized by a technocratic form of governance. Political leaders in Western countries also have less real power to impact the society they are set to govern, and rule in a kind of void (Innset, 2020).

If sustainability is about reusing more and throwing away less, then we must become serious about using local resources and solving tasks more locally, rather than in a centralized manner. For example, social sustainability could mean that local youth or businesses get to participate in the upgrading of municipal properties, and that challenges are solved locally rather than centrally by large companies with administrative capacity, excessive quality and compliance systems, and legal teams. Circular systems mean that public organizations could collaborate with social entrepreneurs and non-profit organizations that create social and environmental sustainability effects locally, that they reuse and repair instead of buying new. Examples could be composting and cultivating locally, reusing building materials, and repairing old doors. We are far from organizing more circularly in this way. Laws, rules, taxes, subsidies, and other incentives do not encourage it. The authorities provide few incentives to help people behave more sustainably, and it is still cheapest to buy new standardized products in large quantities.

THE EARTH CHARTER

Do we need to think differently to behave differently? The Earth Charter may represent another way of thinking about sustainability that is interesting to consider. It arose as a civil society initiative in 2000, and was preceded by the *Our Common Future* report from 1987, led by the then Norwegian prime minister Gro Harlem Brundtland (King, 2010). From the beginning, the initiative was endorsed by institutions and international organizations like UNESCO, which supported its contents and incorporated it as an educational tool in international projects (Hinojosa-Pareja et al., 2014). The Earth Charter pushes the ideas in the Bruntland report further, urging citizens to think globally and act locally for sustainable development (Bosselmann, 2004, 2022). In this era of increasing globalization, the world needs a "charter of global ethics" (Wierzbicka, 2015). The Earth Charter proposes such a global ecological ethics framework of responsibility for "a sustainable global society founded on respect for nature, universal human rights, economic justice and a culture of peace"[1] (Attfield, 2007).

The Rio Earth Summit was held in June 1992 and was attended by 10,000 delegates from 178 countries, resulting in the aforementioned treaties on climate change and biodiversity, the Rio Declaration (Earth

---

[1] https://earthcharter.org/read-the-earth-charter/preamble/

Charter), and a detailed action plan titled *Agenda 21* (Selman, 1993). The writing of this charter was supposed to prepare for the Earth Summit, but an intergovernmental agreement was not achieved, and the Earth Charter ended up as a civil society initiative instead. The official launch of the Earth Charter was held at the Palace of Peace in The Hague on June 29, 2000. The principle of sustainable development was expressed both in the Earth Charter and *Agenda 21*, and was approved at the UN Conference on Environment and Development (UNCED) in Rio de Janeiro in June 1992 (Phan et al., 2022).

The Earth Charter contains a Preamble, where two fundamental statements are found: (a) that "we are one human family" and (b) "one Earth community." The Earth Charter also has 16 interdependent principles organized into four sections or chapters with four principles each and 61 subprinciples in total, which specify these principles, and a final section as an Epilogue. The four main sections or chapters are as follows: (1) Respect and Care for the Community of Life (this is the most important one), (2) Ecological Integrity, (3) Social and Economic Justice, and (4) Democracy, Nonviolence and Peace. The first is a scientific truth because we are genetically a single human species. It is also a legal truth because it is based on the Universal Declaration of Human Rights. Central to the Earth Charter is placing focus on the community in all its diversity. The respect for Earth and life, and the protection of the environment are prerequisites for a just, peaceful, and sustainable global society (Rota et al., 2023). The Earth Charter's three basic principles stress planetary human identity, co-responsibility, and compassion. The first requires that we incorporate nature into education and identity construction, the second entails doing no harm to humans, other living things, and nature, and the third involves training the capability for compassion (Ángeles Murga-Menoyo, 2009).

The ecological perspective embodied in the Earth Charter has a spiritual core emphasizing mindfulness about how your life affects other human beings and other beings, including natural habitats and Earth itself (King, 2010). King (2010) speaks about the importance of acquiring Earth and spiritual literacy, saying that we have extended the power of our human capabilities with machines, telescopes, cellphones, radio, computers, and automation, but must also extend our hearts, love, and soul to the whole human family and planet. This is linked to religious insights. The essence in many of the world's religions is that we are all one, the whole of humanity, including the planet. As humans, we have been too focused on the material and economic dimensions, but development must also be spiritual. To develop the spiritual aspect of human existence, we need fundamental changes in our values, institutions, and ways of living. The Earth Charter therefore underlines that sustainability education, as moral and spiritual education is important for sustainable living. The whole planet and all life can be understood as a vast ecosystem, as described by the Norwegian philosopher Arne Næss in his deep ecological movement (Næss, 1990). He brings together practical environmental concerns with deeply spiritual issues (King, 2010). We need to create the right relationship with ourselves, other people and cultures, and nature. Humans are called to raise their consciousness to reach a higher moral ground. We have to save the world in which we live to save ourselves (King, 2010).

King (2010) refers to spiritual literacy as a deep dimension of insight and wisdom that grows from both the heart and the head. It helps us engage in deep-felt compassion and love for all life. Spiritual literacy does not just evolve by itself, but needs to be fostered and nurtured to grow. For this, spiritual education is needed at all levels, in homes, schools, and colleges. Spiritual education has to reach far beyond the formal world of education and become an integral part of life-long learning. This way of engaging with life must also be adopted by our institutions and organizations. The Earth Charter should be used in education, but above all, it is a moral education of citizens to contribute to sustainable development (Murga-Menoyo, 2009). This education needs to be reflected in the way we organize society, which is not very sustainable today. Some cultures still live in harmonic relationship with nature, and these can be used as an educational resource for sustainable development with the Earth Charter as a basis (Cutanda & Murga-Menoyo, 2014).

Western legal traditions regard humanity as the central and most important element of existence. This puts the legal tradition in opposition to ecological principles (Bosselmann, 2004). At the same time, the ecological crisis worldwide has given rise to the call for everyone to work together to start caring about our natural environment (Chibuye & Buitendag, 2020). Sustainable development can be interpreted as a way of developing human society that reconciles economic growth and social progress with the preservation of the environment to meet the needs of future generations (Phan et al., 2022). An important challenge to the implementation of the Earth Charter has been the operationalization of sustainable development, and the roles and contributions of stakeholders, but also how to change management and governance systems to achieve sustainability, and strategies to ensure local, national, and global sustainability.[2]

Challenges are many and call for a far more collaborative and transdisciplinary problem-solving. We see ecological degradation, an unbalanced distribution of wealth locally and globally, and unsustainable consumer practices, just to mention a few of the deep problems humanity needs to solve. A change in social values to support actions for sustainable development is needed to make fundamental changes, and such values are provided in the Earth Charter (Ahmad et al., 2012).

In one way or another, the Earth as an ecological system has been the core concern of modern international environmental law since its conceptualization in the 1970s. These notions have remained without tangible results. Still, there is a prevailing faith in and the belief that science and technology will result in the continuous improvement of human welfare. Fifty years after the 1972 United Nations Conference on the Human Environment (UNCHE), we can only conclude that international environmental law (IEL) and governance have failed (Ahmad et al., 2012; Bosselmann, 2022).

In the Judeo-Christian tradition, man is set apart from nature and called to dominate. Oriental religions are more holistic and consider humans as an integral part of nature. The Earth Charter combines these two views to balance the respect for nature and for human needs, respecting that primary human needs must be met first (Bourdeau, 2004). This entails that the culture of rampant consumerism has to be replaced by a focus on well-being that encompasses more than material wealth (Buitendag, 2023). Many problems we face are ethical. Therefore, we must imaginatively develop and apply the vision of a sustainable way of life locally, nationally, regionally, and globally, and the Earth Charter can be a valuable resource to do this (Corcoran, 2002). In order to create a post-neoliberal society, we need to change the way we look at the world and focus more on the common good (Hinojosa-Pareja et al., 2014). Still, the Earth Charter meets resistance from a number of intellectual positions, including that it does not provide realistic solutions in international relations. The neoliberal paradigm also conflicts with a spiritual perspective on life and the economy (Fernández-Herrería & Martínez-Rodríguez, 2019).

---

[2] Environmental ethics and the earth charter. (1997). *Environmental Ethics* 19(1), 3–4.

A fundamental restructuring of politics, governance, education, religion, and financial arrangements around the globe is needed—we need a new world vision. According to King (2010), to make this transition, we can learn from traditional religions and philosophies, and the wisdom of native peoples, women, and science. There is a convergence between traditional spiritual perspectives with some of the spiritual insights from modern science. Nevertheless, modern scientific knowledge has limitations because it looks at the universe as a collection of objects rather than investigate the presence of a meaningful universe. According to King, the sacred aspect of the universe has to be rediscovered. All things are interconnected and we must embody that in our way of being in the world. We belong to the Earth, but the Earth does not belong to us (King, 2010).

Arne Næss distinguishes between shallow environmentalism and deep ecology. He was influenced by Spinoza, Gandhi, and the Buddha in his teachings, with a strong emphasis on non-violence. Self-realization of all beings is central in his philosophy. All individuals, humans, and non-humans that the universe consists of should realize the meaning of their being (Næss, 1990; King, 2010; Reichborn-Kjennerud, 2023). The concept of ecological integrity is deeply embedded within the Earth Charter. The continued well-being of humanity depends on the ecological integrity of various natural processes known as Earth's life support systems (Mackey, 2004).

Ideas and beliefs can change the world. Ideas that seem impossible today may one day become politically inevitable (Bregman, 2017). The principles of the Earth Charter can therefore potentially help the transformation of the political, social, and economic orders. It calls for a new and more complex worldview, and for the reintegration of scientific and humanistic culture (Moraes & Petraglia, 2021). Economic, ecological, social, and spiritual well-being need to be included in our understanding of sustainability (Tucker, 2014).

Neoliberalism, as an organizing principle, has produced a series of social, cultural, economic, and personal transformations that have been grouped, since the 1980s, under the term globalization. With neoliberalism, we have gotten markedly more unequal societies. We feel there are no alternatives to its principles, which are grounded in egos' self-interest. This transformation is so dominant that we have gone from a market economy to a market society, where market logic pervades everything. We have privatized social services and state companies, health, education, culture, and knowledge—everything has become merchandise. We therefore need a shift in the way we see the world that can help us in the transition towards an ecological economy and society. We need a new vision as an inspiration and motivation (King, 2010).

Inequality is increasing rapidly and represents a threat to democracies. The corruption of capitalism produces social instability and increasingly corrupt democracies when wealth captures policy-making. A main problem of the current system is inequality, and the concentration of power among the privileged weakens democracy and the rule of law. The state becomes a puppet in their hands. This is the result of globalization without ethics (Stiglitz, 2012). Seven out of 10 people live in countries where inequality has grown in the last 30 years. Half of the worlds' income is in the hands of the richest 1%, while the other half is distributed among the remaining 99% (Fuentes-Nieva & Galasso, 2014).

The second main problem is environmental, including global warming, climate destabilization, pollution, and the loss of biodiversity. Our current trend will lead to an increase of over three degrees Celsius by the end of this century (King, 2010). We therefore need enough people to care for the global commons, and a new way of seeing. The Earth Charter represents such an alternative. In the Earth Charter, the human being is a custodian and caregiver who has developed emotional, social, ecological, and spiritual intelligence, in addition to high cognitive intelligence. This more caring way of being in the world comes with a sense of belonging to all humanity and all living beings. A philosophy like this can lead us towards a post-neoliberal civilization (Fernández-Herrería & Martínez-Rodríguez, 2017). Similar ideas can be found in Felber's (2019) "economy of the common good," ecofeminism, deep ecology, ethics of care, and indigenist thinking (King, 2010). According to Felber, "none of the economists awarded the Nobel Prize have ever shown that competition is the best method we know" (Felber, 2019). Felber concluded that cooperation is more effective than classical competition, but competition protects old structures of power and preserves the status quo (Fernández-Herrería & Martínez-Rodríguez, 2017). The economy of the common good is an operationalization of the values in the Earth Charter that can help transform practice. A future economy would be circular and see the community of life as an end rather than a means, and politics would be at the service of the common good. Different social movements are rehearsing a reality like this. They open spaces in their local sphere, creating communities of vision. Practicing and living what they want to occur, they are faithful to their mission. Experiences with the potential to transform can emerge from these environments and appear as real possibilities for a post-neoliberal society (Fernández-Herrería & Martínez-Rodríguez, 2017).

Changes We Need to Make

The commons and common goods are important benefits mostly organized as public authorities' responsibility because it is difficult to charge for their use. It is not possible for each individual to create such benefits for themselves. However, the challenge is that everyone must contribute to maintaining common goods either by paying taxes or through other types of effort, such as volunteering. However, not everyone can contribute equally. There will always be free riders, and there are limits to how much individuals will contribute without getting something in return (Ostrom, 1999). The tragedy of the commons is that they can be overused since they do not cost anything for the individual to use. They can degrade as a result. Examples are overfishing and littering in parks. It is possible for individuals to fish too much and to leave the park without cleaning up after themselves because they do not bear the direct cost of overfishing or littering. Typical dangers that threaten common goods can also be privatizing behaviors, as seen by the coastline. Therefore, the question is how we can protect, maintain, and organize the use and access to common goods so that we reap the benefits. According to Ostrom, experience has shown that local organization to protect and maintain common goods often can be more effective than centralized organization and control. She explains the tendency towards centralized control from a theory that people seek immediate gain and are unwilling to cooperate to achieve long-term benefits. In such an assumption about self-centred behavior, centralized control makes the most sense. At the same time, Ostrom's research shows that self-organized collective action often yields better results for everyone. When participants protect common goods through their own arrangements, they also create a good local environment (Ostrom, 1999).

As a society, Norway has largely prioritized collectivist solutions. We have reasonable and good public transport, and free schools and health services, but in the public sector, control systems of individual and statutory services are prioritized. Other collectivist solutions, provided collectively rather than as services to individuals, are under pressure. This includes libraries—free meeting places for enlightenment, education, and other cultural activities. The library is a good example of a typical common good, on par with open parks, public access to the coastline, and other types of commons that should not cost anything. In 2002, the Ministry of Culture and Church Affairs proposed to relax the requirement that municipalities must have a library, a proposal that was met with massive protest and finally withdrawn. This shows how there is a lack of incentives and understanding for why and how such common goods are important (Vårheim, 2007).

The Norwegian platform for leadership in the state[3] lists 13 different values that should underpin leadership in public administration. Democracy (popular rule), participation, co-determination, community responsibility, and user orientation are on the list, along with the efficient use of resources in line with political goals. The question is whether the implementation of NPM has allowed equal emphasis on all these values, or whether the focus on efficiency and goal management comes at the expense of and overrides other values. Community is an important human need and central to social well-being. Pricing per unit and counting the number of production and time units do not create the motivation to build and strengthen the commons and community. Counting units makes it harder to finance a new Hyde Park—or the Norwegian equivalent, Vigeland park. The alternative cost of a park is densely built apartment blocks that generate income for developers. This way of constructing reality also makes it harder for homecare workers to sit with users for a cup of coffee when they help clean the older people's home. Life between the houses has little value in this system.

The starting point for the NPM-inspired reforms was to deliver more and better services to the population in a more efficient way—cheaper without compromising quality. Research has shown that this promise has not been fulfilled (Hood & Dixon, 2015). At the same time, control comes at the expense of leadership in the public sector, and there is less room to lead. Management ends up securing compliance with contracts and ensuring that detailed goals and regulations are followed (Falkum, 2020). The demand for control and surveillance grows and has generated its own market fuelled by experts providing their input and advice for more regulation to reduce risk and security gaps. Technology companies, lawyers, consulting and auditing firms offer pseudo-solutions to handle this perceived risk (Falkum et al., 2022; Kuldova, 2022).

[3] https://www.regjeringen.no/no/dokumenter/plattform-for-ledelse-i-staten/id526203/

Regulation has given capital interests an easier playing field. As seen throughout this book, in NPM, the tasks that were previously done in-house are increasingly outsourced to private companies. Developers have more power and key roles in urban planning, while state employees procure instead of doing the job themselves. Procurement is centralized and increasingly larger tenders are announced. Often, only a few big companies have the capacity to send proposals and meet the requirements in public tenders, making it difficult, as a public organization, to buy from smaller businesses and start-ups. At the same time, this contract management generates economic transaction costs—so-called red tape—that are not counted in and create dissatisfaction and stress.

Anxiety and depression are major societal problems, but we promote organizational solutions in working life that stimulate stress. Recent research on the effect of meditation and on altered states of consciousness shows that we have the potential to live and think differently and more peacefully than we do today, but we might then have to govern and organize ourselves in a different way. Taking public health considerations and prioritizing the commons to promote well-being is perhaps something that should be reflected in the way we plan society (Wolf & Abell, 2003). Could municipal community planning contribute to environments that support such calming effects? Could knowledge about human needs and well-being help us see what it takes to create good and harmonious local communities? More peaceful conditions based on cooperation rather than control can be experienced through moods that people pick up socially and unconsciously. Positive moods can influence both individuals and groups. It is not just about whether the bench is freshly painted that matters, but also the atmosphere that is created in a complexly interwoven social system. Creating common arenas with activities and a low threshold for participation can, in this sense, be economically, environmentally, and socially sustainable.

Hardin theorized about the tragedy of the commons, that the commons will always be worn down because people have much to gain and little to lose by overusing them. His solution was state control or to privatize the commons so they are no longer a common good. Ostrom contested this theory and Hardin finally agreed that his assumption was wrong. People can work together to find solutions to organize shared resources in a sustainable way without centralized control. It takes time to develop well-functioning rules and effort to implement and maintain such a system, but people are neither angels nor devils, and are shaped by their institutional context. If institutional conditions promote trust and reciprocity, then people can share common goods without breaking them down, and simultaneously build up a good local environment (Ostrom, 2008). Future public institutions may perhaps play on this dynamic of trust, which we now see a want for through demands for a trust reform in Norway (Johnsen & Svare, 2024).

This book started with a desire to explain how today's governance system is in conflict with sustainable development. The question whether we could take back power from the systems to create a more sustainable society was raised. Hopefully the book has demonstrated, in a balanced way, how New Public Management, as a series of reform measures to open the public sector as a market, from the 1970s, has been taken too far in the direction of control, standardization, and competition. NPM creates more negative bureaucracy and less well-being among citizens, employees, workers, students, residents, and others. A number of concrete examples were given from urban development and various sectors on how this governance system has played out in practice. The book has also entertained thoughts about alternatives that could result in new forms of governance of society giving more power to citizens and protecting the planet at the same time. If public authorities succeed in listening to the needs of citizens, help their initiatives, and build community arenas for cooperation and creative expression, it might help create the sustainable cities we want for the future.

References

Ahmad, W., et al. (2012). Strategic thinking on sustainability: Challenges and sectoral roles. *Environment, Development and Sustainability, 14*(1), 67–83. https://doi.org/10.1007/s10668-011-9309-5

Ángeles Murga-Menoyo, M. (2009). The Earth Charter. A reference for the decade of education for sustainable development. *Revista de Educacion, 239*–262.

Attfield, R. (2007). Beyond the Earth Charter: Taking possible people seriously. *Environmental Ethics, 29*(4), 359–367. https://doi.org/10.5840/enviroethics200729439

Bosselmann, K. (2004). In search of global law: The significance of the Earth Charter. *Worldviews: Environment, Culture, Religion, 8*(1), 62–75. https://doi.org/10.1163/1568535041337766

Bosselmann, K. (2022). Human rights and responsibilities towards the earth system. *Environmental Policy and Law, 52*(3–4), 213–222. https://doi.org/10.3233/EPL-219032

Bourdeau, P. (2004). The man-nature relationship and environmental ethics. *Journal of Environmental Radioactivity, 72*(1–2), 9–15. https://doi.org/10.1016/S0265-931X(03)00180-2

Bregman, A. (2017).

Buitendag, J. (2023). New lenses for a new future. Why science needs theology and why theology needs science. *Hts Teologiese Studies-Theological Studies, 79*(1). https://doi.org/10.4102/hts.v79i1.8191

Chibuye, L., & Buitendag, J. (2020). The indigenisation of eco-theology: The case of the Lamba people of the Copperbelt in Zambia. *Hts Teologiese Studies-Theological Studies, 76*(1). https://doi.org/10.4102/hts.v76i1.6067

Corcoran, P. B. (2002). The values of the Earth Charter in education for sustainable development. *Australian Journal of Environmental Education, 18*, 77–80. https://doi.org/10.1017/S0814062600001154

Cutanda, G. A., & Murga-Menoyo, M. A. (2014). Analysis of mythical-metaphorical narratives as a resource for education in the principles and values of sustainability. *Journal of Teacher Education for Sustainability, 16*(2), 18–38. https://doi.org/10.2478/jtes-2014-0009

Falkum, E. (2020). *Makt og opposisjon i arbeidslivet: Maktforskyvninger fra 1900 til 2020*. Cappelen Damm Akademisk.

Falkum, E., Nordrik, B., Wathne, C. T., Drange, I., Hansen, P. B., Dahl, E. M., Kuldova, T., & Underthun, A. (2022). *Måling og styring av arbeidstid– Medbestemmelsesbarometeret 2021*. AFI-rapport 2022, 01.

Felber, C. (2019). *Change everything: Creating an economy for the common good*. Zed Books Ltd..

Fernández-Herrería, A., & Martínez-Rodríguez, F. M. (2019). The Earth Charter as a new worldview in a post-neoliberal world: Chaos Theory and Morphic Fields as explanatory contexts. *World Futures, 75*(8), 591–608. https://doi.org/10.1080/02604027.2019.1634417

Fuentes-Nieva, R., & Galasso, N. (2014). *Working for the few: Political capture and economic inequality* (Vol. 178). Oxfam.

Hinojosa-Pareja, E. F., et al. (2014). The Earth Charter in compulsory education from an international perspective. *Convergencia-Revista De Ciencias Sociales, 21*(66), 65–92.

Hood, C., & Dixon, R. (2015). *A government that worked better and cost less? Evaluating three decades of reform and change in UK central Government*. Oxford University Press. https://doi.org/10.1093/acprof:oso/9780199687022.001.0001

Innset, O. (2020). *Markedsvendingen: Nyliberalismens historie i Norge*. Fagbokforlaget.

Johnsen, Å., & Svare, H. (2024). *Tillitsreformer og tillitsbasert styring og ledelse*. Fagbokforlaget.

King, U. (2010). Earthing spiritual literacy: How to link spiritual development and education to a new Earth consciousness? *Journal of Beliefs & Values-Studies in Religion & Education, 31*(3), 245–260. https://doi.org/10.1080/1361767 2.2010.520998

Kuldova, T. Ø. (2022). *Compliance-industrial complex: The operating system of a pre-crime society.* Palgrave Pivot. https://doi.org/10.1007/978-3-031-19224-1

Mackey, B. G. (2004). The Earth Charter and ecological integrity—Some policy implications. *Worldviews: Environment, Culture, Religion, 8*(1), 76–92. https://doi.org/10.1163/1568535041337711

Moraes, M. C., & Petraglia, I. (2021). Epistemology of the homeland earth for a new planetary citizenship. *Eccos-Revista Científica, 57.*

Næss, A. (1990). *Ecology, community and lifestyle: Outline of an ecosophy.* Cambridge University Press. https://doi.org/10.1017/CBO9780511525599

Ostrom, E. (1999). Coping with tragedies of the commons. *Annual Review of Political Science, 2*(1), 493–535. https://doi.org/10.1146/annurev.polisci.2.1.493

Ostrom, E. (2008). Tragedy of the commons. *The New Palgrave Dictionary of Economics, 2,* 1–4. https://doi.org/10.1057/978-1-349-95121-5_2047-1

Phan, D., et al. (2022). The position of the sustainable development principle in the legal order of the Czech Republic and in the framework of the Vietnam Act on environmental protection. *Inzynieria Mineralna-Journal of the Polish Mineral Engineering Society,* (1), 97–106.

Reichborn-Kjennerud, K. (2023). Trivsel og gode levekår gir livskvalitet. *Samfunn og økonomi, 2023*(2), 68–71.

Rota, N., et al. (2023). Introducing children in the primary school to the concept of ecosystem services. *Visions for Sustainability, 2023*(19).

Selman, P. (1993). Planning post-Rio. *Planner, 79*(5), 17–19.

Stiglitz, J. E. (2012). *The price of inequality: How today's divided society endangers our future.* WW Norton & Company.

Tucker, M. E. (2014). The Earth Charter and 'Journey of The Universe': An integrated framework for biodemocracy. *Zygon, 49*(4), 910–916. https://doi.org/10.1111/zygo.12132

Vårheim, A. (2007). Social capital and public libraries: The need for research. *Library & Information Science Research, 29*(3), 416–428. https://doi.org/10.1016/j.lisr.2007.04.009

Velten, J. (2022). Tillitsbasert leder-og medarbeiderskap. *Stat & Styring, 32*(2), 30–33. https://doi.org/10.18261/stat.32.2.9

Wierzbicka, A. (2015). A charter of global ethics, in Universal Words. *Teksty Drugie,* (4), 257–279.

Wolf, D. B., & Abell, N. (2003). Examining the effects of meditation techniques on psychosocial functioning. *Research on Social Work Practice, 13*(1), 27–42. https://doi.org/10.1177/104973102237471

Index[1]

A
Accountability, 27, 28, 31, 41, 43
Activity-based financing, 26
Administration, 4, 8, 15, 24, 25, 27, 31, 32, 43, 58, 67, 83, 85, 87, 88, 100, 111, 134
Agencies, 4, 15, 23, 24, 29–32, 41, 46, 54, 83, 91, 93, 104, 115, 116
Agency theory, 24
Agenda 21, 10, 99, 128
Airbnb, 85, 118, 119
Alternative visions, 5
Anxiety, 135
Area-based initiative, 81, 82, 94, 95, 101, 114–116, 121, 122
Authoritarian, 42

B
Barriers for cooperation, 8
Best practice guidelines, 8, 54

Biological diversity, 10
Bourdieu, Pierre, 75, 76, 80, 81
Brazil, 10
Brundtland, Gro Harlem, 127
Brundtland Commission, 9, 10
Buddha, 131
Bureaucracy, 4, 8, 23, 31, 32, 54, 77, 88, 136
Bureaucratization, 23
Business accounting, 30

C
Capitalism, 32, 53, 132
Capitalist realism, 3, 11
Cash accounting, 30
Central city districts, 85
Centralization, 28, 29, 54, 99–104
Circular systems, 103, 126–127
Civil servants, 31
Civil society, 17, 24, 66, 80, 127, 128

---

[1] Note: Page numbers followed by 'n' refer to notes.

Climate footprint, 4, 14
Co-creation, 17–19, 25, 79, 92–98, 110
Co-determination, 43, 60, 68, 87, 134
Co-governance, 17
Collective action, 133
Collective interest, 42
Commercial forces, 18, 120
Common goods, 8, 61, 64, 130, 132–136
Commons, 14, 28, 33, 52, 56, 57, 59, 61–64, 66, 74, 75, 80, 81, 90, 93, 94, 117, 118, 122, 126, 130, 132–136
Community garden, 65, 101, 113, 114
Community planning, 2, 3, 16, 19, 110, 135
Community values, 28, 92, 119
Compact city, 73
Compact urban development, 4, 74
Competition, 3, 5, 8, 16, 22, 23, 26, 32, 38, 42, 45–48, 55, 58, 100–102, 104, 126, 132, 136
Competitive tendering, 26
Compliance, 12, 23, 24, 41, 55, 127, 134
  audits, 24
Concept of sustainability, 8, 9, 11, 12, 14, 55, 56
Conflicts of interest, 25
Consumption, 8, 14, 99, 99n2, 100, 104
Context-dependent, 15, 17, 29
Contract management, 4, 22, 28, 34, 135
Contracts, 4, 8, 23–27, 29, 32, 44–48, 53, 61, 68, 100, 101, 103, 104, 111, 126, 134, 135
Control, 3, 5, 7, 8, 18, 19, 22–24, 26–32, 38, 40–45, 47, 48, 54, 55, 75, 77, 87, 104, 117, 120, 126, 133–136
  procedures, 44

Cooperation, 5, 7, 8, 16, 24, 32, 42, 65, 66, 74, 75, 116, 126, 132, 135, 136
Cost-benefit, 12
Cost control, 8, 26, 31, 40, 54, 77
Cost-cutting, 3, 5
Creativity, 5, 8
Cross-sectoral, 14, 15, 29, 100
Cultural capital, 76, 82, 85
Curiosity, 39

D
Decentralization, 28
Decision-making processes, 17
Deep ecological movement, 129
Democracy, 3, 5, 25, 27, 34, 53–56, 58, 60–62, 64, 66, 67, 80, 87–90, 96, 111, 126, 128, 132, 134
Democratic urban development in the digital age (DEMUDIG), 52, 57, 58, 65, 67, 77, 81, 83, 85–87, 89–92, 96, 98
Densification, 5, 52, 57–60, 63, 66, 78, 93, 111, 122
  policy, 52, 57–60, 66, 111, 122
Depression, 135
Developers, 4, 18, 25, 52, 53, 56–61, 63, 64, 74, 75, 82, 84, 111, 121, 134, 135
Developing countries, 9, 17
Development, 4, 7–19, 23, 26, 28, 34, 39, 40, 43, 51–53, 55–58, 60, 61, 63–68, 74–94, 98–101, 109–111, 116, 120–122, 125–130, 136
Digitalization, 43, 117
Digital participation, 67
Digitization, 43, 48, 54, 102
Discretion, 27, 28, 32, 43, 55
Discursive space, 75, 76
Districts, 15, 56–58, 65, 82–86, 91–93, 95, 102, 114, 119, 121, 122

Diversity, 41, 61, 84, 101, 121, 128
Documentation, 24
DRG system, 27
Drucker, P., 42

E
Earth Charter, 127–133
Ecological perspective, 128
Economic growth, 9, 63, 98, 129
EdiCitNet, 65, 102, 112–114
Education, 4, 5, 27, 28, 33, 37–48, 90, 111, 126, 128, 129, 131, 133
Efficiency, 3, 5, 6, 22, 26, 28, 48, 62, 77, 80, 111, 126, 134
Employment services, 40
Entrepreneurial cities, 60–63
Environment, 55, 56, 64, 66, 68, 74, 76, 79, 80, 82, 93, 98, 99, 111, 128, 129, 133, 135, 136
Environmental sustainability, 6, 13, 74, 78, 98, 126, 127
EU, 47
Evaluation, 44, 45, 78
Expertise, 15, 34, 54, 64, 68
Expert knowledge, 43
External motivation, 39

F
Financial crisis, 40
Financial regulations, 26, 58
Flexibility, 8, 32, 96
Florida, Richard, 60, 63, 76
Food, 4, 13–15, 47, 101–104
Formalization, 41, 44
Fragmented public organizations, 19
Framework agreements, 45, 47, 101, 102
Fredrikstad, 10
Funding, 44, 45
Future generations, 9, 12, 56, 129

G
Gaming the numbers, 8
Gentrification, 2, 3, 53, 60, 62, 63, 66, 74, 81, 86, 92, 95, 96, 118
Glass, Ruth, 63
Governance, 2, 3, 14, 16, 17, 23–26, 29–32, 51–68, 73, 77–80, 120–122, 126, 130, 131, 136
of the public sector, 77, 79
Government, 7, 8, 10, 11, 22, 22n1, 27, 31, 33, 89
Governmentality, 55
Growth, 4, 8, 9, 14, 24, 42, 63, 77, 98–100, 117, 129
mindset, 39

H
Health trusts, 40
Healy, Patsy, 66
Higher education, 44
Holistic thinking, 5, 12, 16, 19
Hood, Christopher, 22, 23, 26, 27, 37, 134
Human rights, 14, 16, 127
Hybrid organizational forms, 23

I
Incentives, 8, 22–24, 101, 112, 127, 134
Incentive schemes, 26, 29, 44
Inclusion, 13, 79, 94
Inclusive planning processes, 17
Individualization, 5, 23, 40, 62, 126
Industrialization, 8, 32, 53
Inequality, 8, 34, 110, 121, 132
Inequality-creating systems, 11
Innovation, 2, 4, 8, 17, 44, 45, 101, 102, 117
Interdisciplinary, 2
Internal competition, 38

Internal motivation, 39
Internal pricing, 26, 29
Internationalization, 23
Investors, 11, 74, 75, 77, 126

J
Jacobs, Jane, 65
Johannesburg, 10

K
Key indicator thinking, 5

L
Labor market, 28, 33, 34, 39
Large companies, 23, 100, 101, 127
Leadership, 22, 40, 43, 99, 134
Letters of allocation, 26, 31
Libraries, 52, 61, 63, 94, 112, 117, 118, 133, 134
Liveable places, 18
Living conditions, 15, 17, 55, 66, 74, 79, 81, 82, 84, 86, 93, 117, 118, 121, 122
Local community, 10, 13, 15, 17, 51, 56, 58, 60, 64–66, 78, 80, 81, 83, 86, 87, 89, 92, 95–97, 99, 101, 112–117, 122, 126, 135
Local democracy, 3, 64, 80, 87, 111

M
Madrid, 58, 85, 87–90, 93, 118, 119
Management by Objectives and Results (MBOR), 16, 18, 22, 23, 26, 39, 42, 43, 54, 77, 78, 110, 126
Market principles, 8, 31, 32
Market solutions, 4, 32
Material space, 74–76, 82, 83

Melbourne, 57, 58, 87–90, 93, 119
Mental health, 39, 97, 113
Metrics, 8, 28
Micro-management, 54
Millennium Development Goals, 11
Ministries, 23, 24, 26, 29, 32, 122
Modernization, 3, 32
Monopolization, 48, 101
Motivation, 39–45, 90, 132, 134
Municipalities, 4, 5, 8, 10, 12–19, 29, 46, 47, 52, 53, 56, 57, 60, 61, 63, 67, 75, 77–79, 81, 83–85, 88, 89, 93, 97–99, 101–104, 110–118, 121, 125, 134

N
Næss, Arne, 129, 131
Nature, 3, 6, 9, 25, 28, 42, 65, 79, 98, 100, 115, 119, 122, 127–130
Neighborhood association, 119
Neoliberal, 3, 26, 42, 58, 63, 66, 77, 79, 98, 117, 120, 126, 130
New Public Management (NPM), 2–6, 17, 21–24, 26–34, 37–48, 51–68, 77, 109, 116, 126, 134–136
New York, 11, 62
Non-profit organizations, 45, 46, 79, 83, 100, 127

O
Office of the Auditor General (OAG), 24
Old Public Management (OPM), 26, 31, 32, 77
Organic production, 104
Organization for Economic Cooperation and Development (OECD), 22, 22n1, 38, 45
Organization-specific goals, 28

Oslo, 5, 15, 51–53, 56–58, 63, 67, 85–89, 92, 93, 97, 114, 116, 117, 119, 122
Ostrom, E., 133, 135, 136
Outcome, 18, 25, 33, 44, 76, 87
Output, 33
Outsourcing, 26, 29, 38, 48
Over-implementation, 24

P

Parks, 16, 28, 56, 57, 61–63, 74, 75, 86, 95, 112, 114, 115, 133, 134
Participation, 2–6, 17, 25, 27, 32, 40–46, 53, 56–61, 64–68, 74, 78, 79, 82, 84, 85, 87–91, 94, 99, 111, 121, 134, 135
Performance measurement, 28
Planning, 2, 3, 5, 8, 12, 16, 17, 19, 34, 52, 57, 59–61, 64–68, 74, 78, 79, 81, 89, 91, 93, 99, 110, 111, 120, 121, 126, 135
Planning and Building Act, 5, 12, 58, 59, 78, 110, 111
Plastic, 13
Policy areas, 38, 126
Political, 2–4, 13, 31, 43, 52, 56, 64, 77, 80, 84, 85, 87, 89, 93, 111, 120, 121, 126, 131, 134
  science, 2, 3
Post-neoliberal society, 130, 133
Poverty, 9, 10, 96
Power imbalances, 25, 67
Principal, 24
Private developers, 4, 57, 59
Procurement rules, 4
Procurement unit, 47
Production, 5, 13, 14, 26, 28, 38–48, 53, 63, 76, 77, 99, 126, 134
Productivity, 42, 60
Professional discretion, 27, 32, 43, 55

Profit, 4–6, 30, 52–54, 57, 63, 66, 74, 81, 111, 120
Project grants, 114
Property owners, 53, 75
Proposals, 45, 59, 61, 84, 85, 90, 91, 114, 134, 135
Public enterprises, 16, 18, 22, 27, 29, 30, 32
Public good, 3, 5, 38, 62
Public health, 4, 12, 34, 42, 55, 78, 110–113, 118, 122, 125, 135
Public procurement, ix, 4, 5, 13, 37–48, 104
Public service delivery, 17
Purchaser-provider model, 4
Putnam, Robert, 75, 80

Q

Quality, ix, 2–4, 13, 17, 24, 26, 27, 33, 34, 38, 40–45, 47, 53, 61, 66, 74, 78, 101, 111, 126, 127, 134
  assurance, 40, 44
  reform, 44
  systems, 4, 100
Quasi-contracts, 23

R

Recycle, 58
Red tape, 24, 41, 135
Regulation, 3, 4, 23, 24, 26, 31, 38, 42–44, 47, 55, 58, 75, 77, 82, 83, 103, 119, 126, 134, 135
Regulatory state, 4, 23, 41, 59
Reporting, 8, 11, 12, 18, 23, 24, 44, 54
Research, ix, 4, 5, 26, 27, 34, 39, 44, 45, 52, 54, 57, 61, 63, 65n4, 79–81, 83, 102, 133–135
Residents' needs, 15, 83

Responsive, 18, 54, 91, 115
Result units, 26, 29, 116
Reuse, 103, 115, 116, 127
Reward mechanisms, 26
Right to the city, 62
Rigid service provision, 38
Rio conference, 10
Risk, 3, 5, 9, 25, 40, 42, 44, 54, 89, 100, 101, 103, 116, 121, 134

S
School, 27, 29, 33, 38–48, 79, 81, 85, 94, 95, 97, 98, 102, 111, 113, 115, 129, 133
Scientific management, 32
Segregation, 68
Sense of belonging, 17, 78, 132
Silo tendencies, 15
Small-and medium-sized companies, 45
Smart cities, 66, 74
Social capital, 2, 3, 56, 74–76, 78, 80–82, 85, 94, 98, 119
Social city life, 117
Social cohesion, 3, 65, 85, 92
Social entrepreneurs, 79, 95–98, 100, 101, 114, 127
Socially sustainable cities, 60
Social meeting places, 17
Social needs, 5
Social networks, 74, 92
Social space, 75, 76, 80–83
Social sustainability, 3, 5, 6, 8, 12, 13, 16–19, 46, 55–58, 64, 66, 67, 74, 75, 77, 78, 82, 83, 86, 102, 111, 126–127
Societal results, 18, 28, 33
Sociology, 3, 117

Spatial planning, 8
Spiritual intelligence, 132
Standardization, 3, 18, 28, 54, 116, 126, 136
Standards, 8, 22, 39
Supervisory bodies, 23
Surveillance, 32, 43, 54, 55, 134
Sustainable Development Goals (SDGs), 2, 8, 11, 12
Sustainable urban transitions, 2
Systemic problems, 14, 116

T
Taxpayer money, 18, 27, 34
Taylor, Frederick, 32
Templates, 44, 45
Tenders, 27, 30, 45–48, 99–101, 103, 104, 135
Threshold values, 47–48
Throughput, 33, 44, 45
Time pressure, 8
Tokenism, 64–65
Tourism, 93
Tøyen, 81, 82, 84, 93–96, 98, 117, 122
Traditional bureaucracy, 32, 77
Transaction costs, 37, 135
Transdisciplinary, 130
Trust, 29, 40, 56, 58, 66, 68, 74, 80, 83, 87–93, 136
    reform, 136

U
UN conference, 10
Unintended consequences, 23, 27, 32–33, 86
Unions, 40, 43, 60
Unit price financing, 26, 27, 29
UN summit, 10

Urban development, 4, 5, 13, 17, 52, 53, 55–61, 64–68, 75–77, 79–93, 98–99, 109, 111, 120–122, 136
Urban governance, 3, 51–68, 77–80, 122
User participation, 17

V
Value, 5, 15, 27, 28, 31, 46, 52, 54, 55, 62, 66, 67, 74, 79, 81, 93, 94, 98, 112, 114, 126, 129, 130, 132, 134
Variation, 41, 117
Voluntary organizations, 17, 18, 83

W
Waste production, 14
Weber, Max, 31, 32
Welfare services, 38
Welfare state, 2, 27
Well-being, 3–5, 17, 38, 40–45, 51, 55, 56, 61, 65, 78, 110, 114, 126, 130, 131, 134–136
Working Environment Act, 44
Working life, 4, 37–48, 88, 135

Z
Zoning plans, 58, 59, 61